I0459866

# PIANO
## COURSE BOOK
### —| FOR BEGINNERS |—

**VIDEO
LESSONS
FALLING
NOTES**

*Teach yourself how to read music, play famous piano songs, educational and methodological manual 140 pieces*

ISBN 979-8-218-63461-2

# FROM THE AUTHOR

"The Course of Piano Playing" is designed for its consistent use in the junior grades of children's music schools: preparatory, first and, partially, second. At the same time, the "Course" can become a desk manual (self-study guide) for music lovers of any age who want to independently acquire basic skills in playing the piano.

When selecting the repertoire of the "Course", the author proceeded from the idea that the musical destiny of a student largely depends on his first pieces played: whether he will love music sincerely and selflessly or share the fate of indifferent and mediocre performers. Therefore, a beginning musician should deal only with musical samples, albeit simple, but in this case capable of causing an elevated emotional state. To satisfy the teachers craving new and intonationally attractive material, the repertoire of the "Course" is made up of works and arrangements of original and folk music from Western European and North American countries, selected by the authors of the "Course" directly in these countries. In the "Course", 140 pieces are included. The author is convinced that when educating a beginning pianist it is necessary to add musical material with an expressive melody, harmonious harmony, clear rhythm, and clear form-building elements to the skill of the teacher and the talent of the student. He was guided by this when compiling the repertoire.

The pieces included in the course are different in character and style, selected with a gradual complication of musical content and playing movements, and completely edited.

The authors considered it appropriate to include several original methodological instructions in the musical text so that when learning the pieces they would be in the student's sphere of attention.

For those who prefer independent learning, the initial sections of the "Course" contain short, original, and effective theoretical material, which at the same time can be useful for teachers of summer music schools.

# TABLE OF CONTENTS

# CHAPTER I

## BEFORE YOU START PLAYING THE PIECES

## TWO FIRST ACQUAINTANCES

Dear friend! Before you sit down at the piano you need to get to know your hands better.

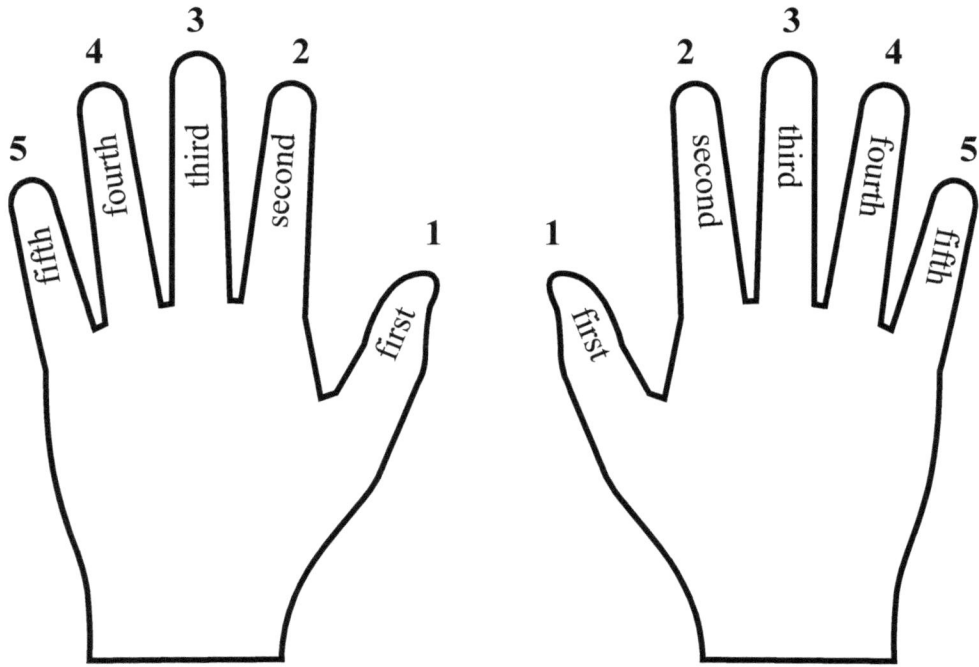

Before getting acquainted wash your hands thoroughly and trim your nails short.

Sit at a table and open a clean school notebook. Place your hands with slightly spread fingers on two open pages. Trace your fingers with a pencil just like in the illustration.

Number all ten fingers and write the name of each one. From this moment on, as a true pianist, each of your fingers will have its own number. The strongest finger - the thumb - will be called "FIRST" and marked with the number "1." The most flexible finger - the index finger - will be called "SECOND" and marked with the number "2." The longest finger - the middle finger - will be called "THIRD" and marked with the number "3." The least agile finger - the ring finger - will be called "FOURTH" and marked with the number "4." The weakest finger - the little finger - will be called "FIFTH" and marked with the number "5." Remember these new names for your fingers, and when you sit at the piano, do not call them anything else.

Now, you need to learn two special and very useful exercises for your hands and fingers.

**Exercise 1.** Stand freely next to the piano, straighten up, and relax the muscles of your shoulders, arms, and fingers. Ideally, relax the muscles of your entire body.

Without moving from your spot, rotate your torso and relaxed arms freely in one direction, then the other. Let your hands, wrists, and fingers naturally wrap around your body as you turn. Repeat this several times. Then, to fully relax your hands, shake your wrists a few times, as if shaking water off them after washing.

**Exercise 2.** Place a chair with a firm or semi-firm seat (a soft one won't work!) in front of the closed piano lid. Sit on the chair and extend your arms forward so that your fingers are just above the center of the lid. Without forcing, curve and round the fingers of your right hand first, then your left hand, as shown in the illustrations.

After you have "gathered" and rounded your fingers, you should bend and straighten them only at the TOP JOINTS.

Do not press your fingers together, make sure they do not "stick" or "cling" to each other - let your fingers have enough space. However, there's no need to spread them too far apart either.

Now, imagine that each of your hands is holding a small Christmas ornament made of very thin glass. You need to gently grasp the ornaments with your fingers and hold them but don't press too hard or strain your fingers - the fragile decorations might shatter. Calmly and slowly, relax your fingers at the top joints. Carefully "place" the ornaments on the piano lid, and with the tips or "pads" of all ten fingers simultaneously, touch the surface of the lid, as shown in the illustration.

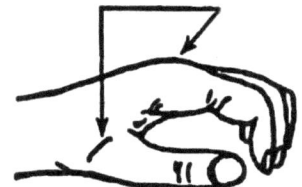

BEND AND UNBEND ONLY HERE!

BEND AND EXTEND YOUR FINGERS ONLY AT THE UPPER JOINTS!

Without changing the position of your wrists (fingers should not "stick together"!), gently press the "pads" of all 10 fingers onto the piano lid and feel how the tips of your fingers rest against its surface. Then, calmly lift your hands back to their original position with freely extended fingers.

Repeat the motion several times: "grasp" the imaginary glass ornaments with the rounded fingers of both hands and "place" them on the piano lid, lightly pressing down.

Make sure to do these two useful exercises every time before sitting down at the piano.

Now, it's time to get acquainted with your piano. Remember that the piano has a second full name - FORTEPIANO. This name comes from two Italian words. The word "forte" means "loud," while "piano" means "soft." It's as if these two words are arguing with each other: "Loud!" exclaims forte, "Soft" whispers - "piano".

You will soon discover why these two words are at odds with each other.

1. Ask someone to help you open the front panel of the piano and open its lid. Under the lid you'll see a long row of WHITE and BLACK keys. Together they are called the KEYBOARD. Look at the keyboard and then compare it to the illustration.

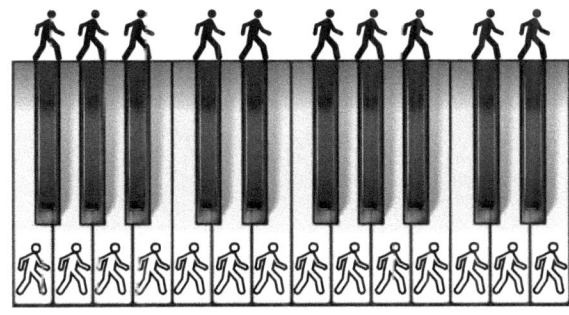

The white keys "march" one by one and strictly one after another and the black ones "go" in companies - TWO and THREE. Why this happens, you will find out a little later.

Right above the keyboard rises a whole forest of STRINGS. And next to the golden and silver strings, soft HAMMERS have frozen. There are also a lot of hammers, because each white and black key has its own hammer.

Look down under the keyboard. At the very bottom you see two pedals - right and left. Sometimes there is a third pedal between them - the middle one. When playing the piano your feet are on the pedals but for now you won't have to use the pedals.

**Remember!** The white key which is located on the keyboard to the left of the two black keys and under which the left pedal is located at the bottom is conventionally considered the MIDDLE key for the entire keyboard.

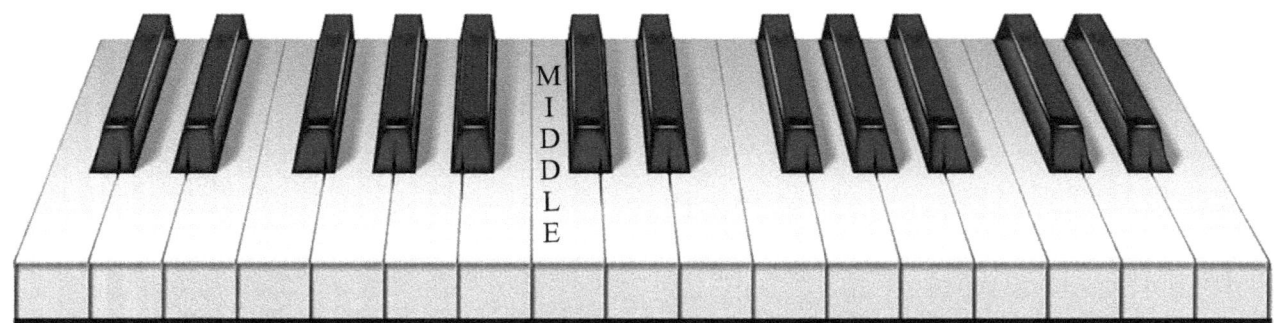

2. Now you need to correctly position the chair you will sit on at the piano. You can have either a regular chair or a round screw-on chair but it must have a hard or semi-hard seat.

The chair should be opposite the middle of the keyboard. An imaginary line drawn through the middle of the chair seat should pass between the piano pedals.

Stretch your right arm straight out in front of you. Move the chair towards the piano so that its back or the back of the round seat of the screw-on chair is approximately at the distance of your outstretched arm from the front edge of the keyboard. Sit on the seat closer to the edge of the chair because when playing the piano you never lean on the back of the chair. Imagine that your fingers are again "holding" glass balls. Stretch both hands forward with rounded fingers. Carefully "place" the balls on the keyboard and touch the middle of the white keys with your fingertips. In this position, you should sit not too close to the keyboard but not too far either. You need to sit at such a DISTANCE and at such a HEIGHT that the lower surfaces of your arms - from your elbows to your hands - are level with the surface of the keys - not HIGHER and not LOWER. Your elbows should also be at this level or slightly higher. The height of the screw-in chair is easy to adjust. But if the chair is regular then you must definitely choose the right height for you. Sit on the chair freely, leaning slightly forward, but do not slouch. Keep your body straight but not tense. If your legs reach the floor then they should stand straight on both sides of the pedals and as close to them as possible. If your legs do not reach the floor you need to choose a suitable stool for them.

3. Sitting on the chair stretch your arms forward. Right above the middle of the free wide part of the white keys, round the fingers of both hands, and again imagine that you are holding fragile glass balls. Do not bend or strain your fingers too much.

Continuing to "hold" the balls lower the *second* fingers down at the same time as in this picture.

Then lift your fingers back to their previous position. The most important thing: while the SECOND fingers are moving down and up the other four fingers move AS LITTLE AS POSSIBLE and continue to "hold" the glass balls. Make sure that your fingers do not "stick together"!

Make the "down and up" movement with your second fingers several times at a speed that is comfortable for you.

Make exactly the same movement with your third fingers several times. Don't forget the main thing: while the THIRD fingers are moving, the other four fingers move AS LITTLE AS POSSIBLE.

Put your hands on your knees and rest a little. Your hands should be completely free and not tense. But they should not be flaccid but ready for action. Make the "down and up" movement with your first, fourth and fifth fingers. Put your hands on your knees and rest again.

4. Calmly remove your left hand from your knee and press the middle key with your third finger. Do it like this: smoothly lower the hand with rounded fingers from above, with the third finger, onto the key, and with the downward movement of the finger that you just did, GENTLY LOWER the key down to the limit, as in this picture.

Look at the finger pressing the key. It is slightly bent and rounded, as if it were still holding the glass ball. But it is not rounded very much. The finger is not at the edge of the white key, but in its MIDDLE, and this means that it is CLOSER to the BLACK keys. The finger presses the key with its very tip - the CUFF. The other fingers are also rounded, as if they are still holding the ball.

And in this picture the finger presses the key incorrectly. Why? Firstly, the third finger pressed the key at its very edge. Because of this, the first finger ended up beyond the edge of the keyboard. Secondly, the third finger did not fully complete the "down" movement that you just learned, and did not go down enough, completely. Because of this, the second finger went down too low, and "hangs", almost touching the keys. Do not make these mistakes and continue to calmly press the key several times.

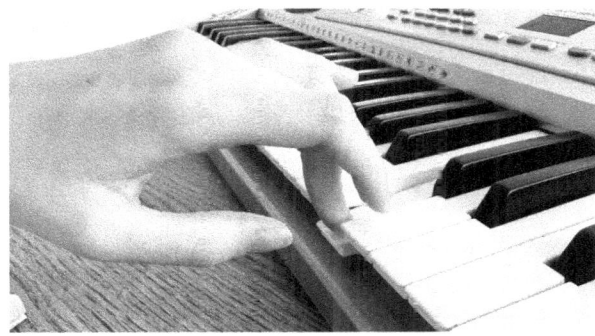

Put your left hand on your knee. With the third finger of your right hand, and then the second and fourth, press the middle key several times. Press with different force and listen to the sounds of the strings.

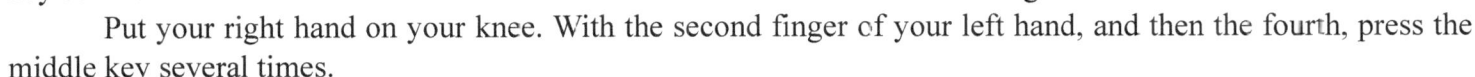

Put your right hand on your knee. With the second finger of your left hand, and then the fourth, press the middle key several times.

Be sure to try pressing the key with different force - sometimes harder, sometimes weaker. Watch how the hammer "works" and strikes the strings. Try to feel well "by ear" how differently the strings sound from strong and weak strokes.

Put both hands on your knees and rest a little.

Pressing the middle key, you, of course, felt that if you press or hit the key HARD, then your stroke will be repeated by the hammer, and the string will sound loudly. If you press the key SOFTLY, without making much effort, then the hammer will hit the string weakly, and the string will sound quietly. The FORTEPIANO is called so because you can play it both LOUDLY and QUIETLY. Then what are these two words arguing about: "forte" - loud, and "piano" - quietly? Press the key hard and sharply and immediately remove your finger from it. In response, the string "screamed" with a sharp, abrupt sound.

Press the same key very lightly and immediately remove your finger from it. This time the sound is quiet, short and not memorable. Press this key with medium force and hold your finger on it for a while before removing it. The sound is smooth, drawn-out and more pleasant to the ear. So this is what the two words "forte" and "piano" argue about. They argue about how to press the keys so that the strings sound the most beautiful. Musicians have understood this for a long time. The sound is the most beautiful when the string "sings" at medium volume with a soft, smooth, melodious "voice". This sound lasts for some time, "hangs" in the air and does not immediately leave the room. To get such a sound, press the keys with medium force, softly and hold your finger on the key for some time.

Ask for help to put the front wall of the piano back in place. Remember that behind it are the strings that you hit with the hammers. The force with which the hammer hits is the volume with which the string will respond.

In music, the volume of a sound is indicated by Italian words:

*Forte*, abbreviated as "F" or "*f*", means "loud", "strong". This means that you should play loudly.

*Fortissimo*, abbreviated as "FF" or "*ff*", means "very strong", "very loud".

*Mezzo-forte*, abbreviated as "Mf" or "*mf*", means "not very loud", "with a medium volume".

*Piano* (pronounced piano), abbreviated as "P" or "*p*", means "quiet". This means that you should play quietly.

*Pianissimo*, abbreviated "PP" or "*pp*", means - "very quiet".

*Mezzo-piano*, abbreviated "Mp" or "*mp*", means - not very quiet, a little quieter than medium volume.

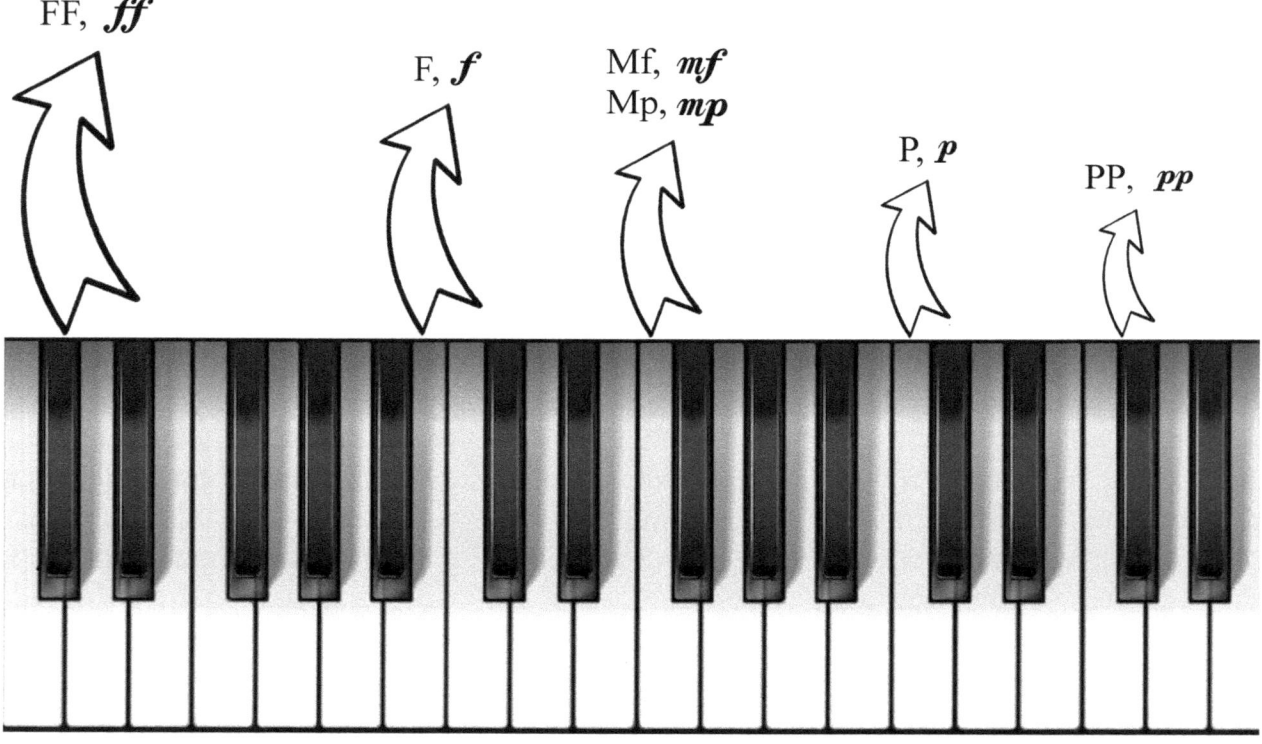

# GET TO KNOW THE PIANO KEYBOARD
# AND THE MAIN MUSICAL SOUNDS

This picture shows the MIDDLE part of the keyboard.

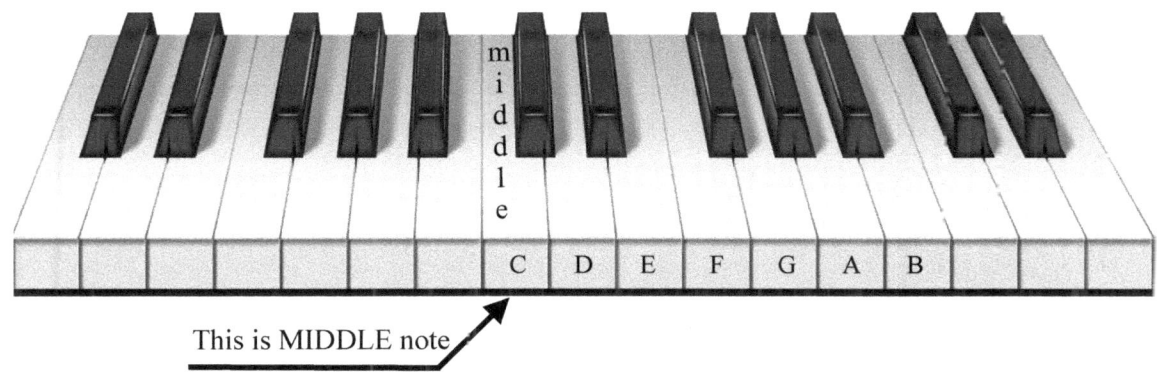

This is MIDDLE note

Starting with the *middle* key, the seven white keys have their names written on them: C, D, E, F, G, A, B. You should know these names by heart from beginning to end and from end to beginning and be able to quickly find these seven keys on the keyboard. The middle key has just received its own name - "C". Therefore, you can call it - C middle or Middle C.

1. Press each of the seven keys with the 2nd or 3rd finger of your right hand, starting with Do middle, and sing its name loudly: "C! D! E! F! G! A! B!" The seven sounds that you hear have the same names as the seven white keys that you see. Try to make your voice completely match each of these seven sounds. Musicians say: "The voice merges with the sound."
If this does not work out right away, do not be upset. SING - and IT WILL CERTAINLY WORK OUT!

Press each of the seven keys in reverse order. Loudly sing the names of the seven sounds and the seven keys: "B! A! G! F! E! D! C!!"

Remember! The SEVEN sounds that you just played and sang are the MAIN sounds in music. The seven keys that you pressed "march" one after another in a long row of white keys. In music, any row of sounds that "march" one after another in a certain order is called a sound series or simply a SOUND SCALE. Therefore, you have now become acquainted with a SOUND SCALE of seven main sounds. This sound series has its own musical name. It is called an OCTAVE, which means "eighth" in Latin. Why eighth? After all, there are only seven sounds - C, D, E, F, G, A, B?

2. Press the key that "marches" immediately after the seventh B key as in this picture.

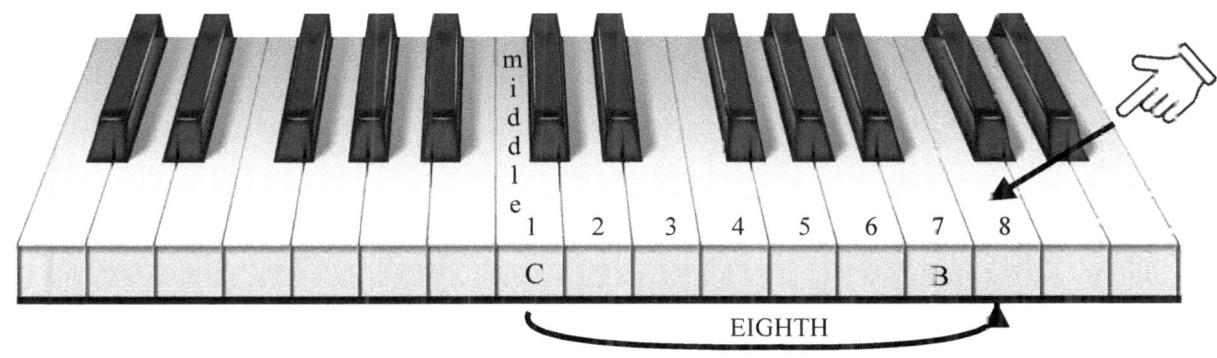

EIGHTH

If you count from the C middle key, this will be the eighth key. Hold your finger on this key and listen to its sound. It seems that this sound is already familiar to you. Press C middle, and then immediately the eighth key. Do this several times until you are convinced "by ear" that these two sounds sound almost the same.

Press these two keys with the fingers of your right and left hand at the same time and listen. You hear one common sound because the two sounds of these keys join into one.

3. Find the eighth keys for the remaining sounds of the octave yourself - for D for E, F for G, A for B. Make sure "by ear" that each eighth key very similarly repeats one of the sounds of the octave - C, D, E, F, G, A, B.

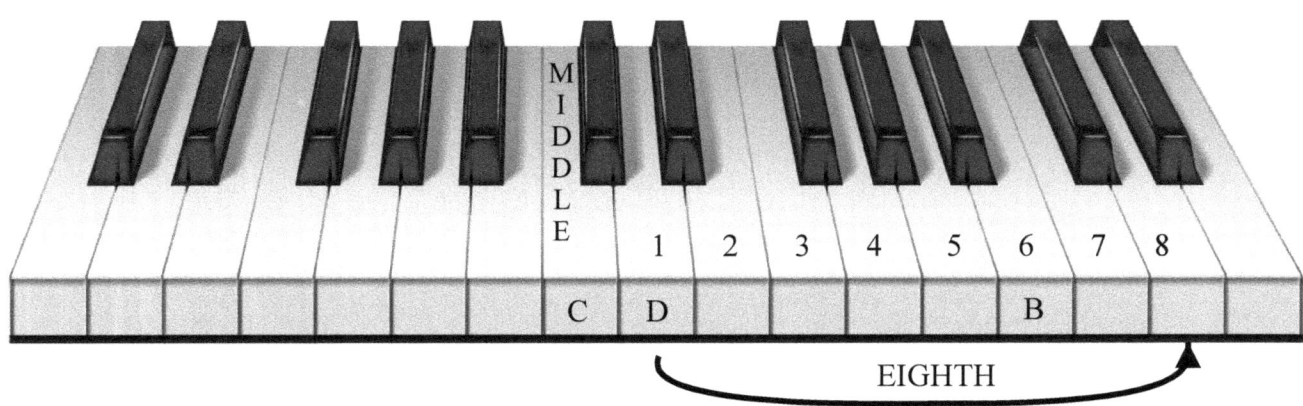

Thus, the main musical sounds - C, D, E, F, G, A, B, are repeated every seven keys. In the entire long scale of white keys there are no other sounds.

Every eighth key repeats the sound of the first. Therefore, the entire keyboard and the entire scale of the piano consist of octaves. You will learn about the black keys that are in each octave a little later.

4. Count on your own how many octaves there are on the right side of the keyboard, starting with the middle C key. It turns out that there are exactly four octaves and one more white C key as in this picture.

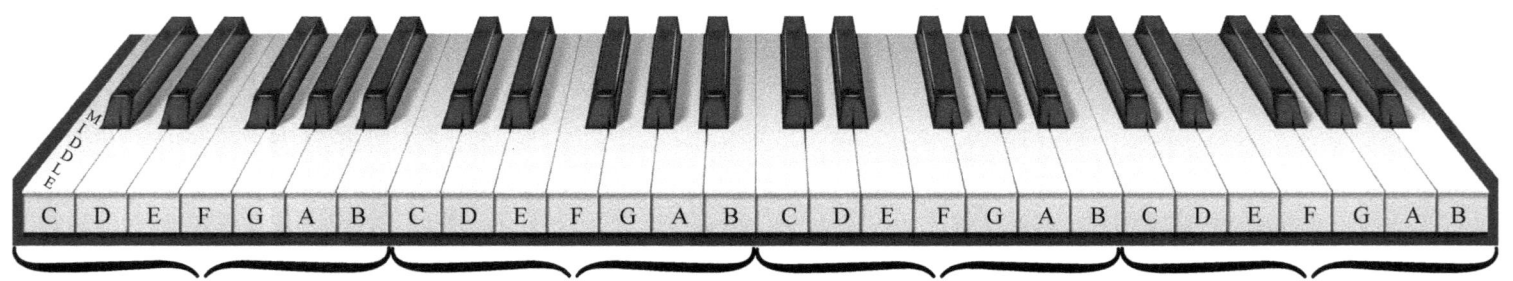

This is the first octave     This is the second octave     This is the third octave     This is the fourth octave

These four octaves are called *First, Second, Third and Fourth*. The names of the sounds and keys are repeated in all four octaves.

The left side of the keyboard is designed exactly the same as the right one. But you will get to know it a little later.

# UNDERSTAND HOW THE OCTAVE IS "STRUCTURED"

Press the keys of the First octave in order with the 2nd or 3rd finger of the Right hand and imagine that you are climbing a white marble staircase. The names of the main sounds of the octave are written on the steps of the staircase. Stepping on a new step with your foot you press a new key and hear a new sound. Feel "by ear" how with each new key and step the sound becomes more tender and subtle. But musicians do not say this, they say - "the sound has become higher." Therefore, it turns out that in each octave the sound of C is the lowest and the highest is the sound of B.

Look at the "sound staircase", the steps of which are built from eight main sounds.

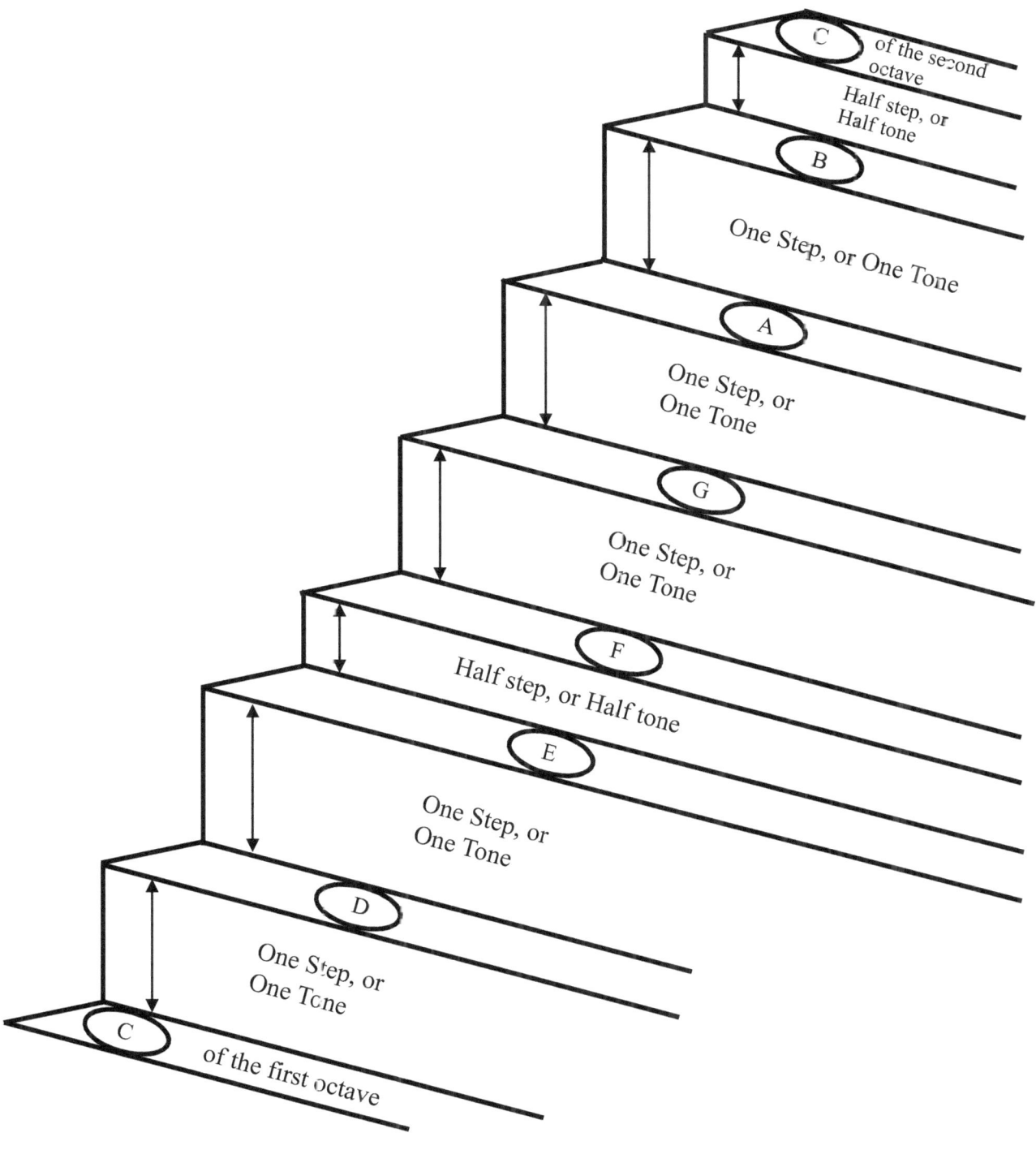

The eight steps are the seven sounds of the first octave and the "marching" sound C of the Second Octave right after them. The "steps" of which the octave is built have different pitches. Between the sounds C and D, between D and E, between F and G, G and A, A and B - there is one step each. But between the sounds E and F, as well as between G and C of the Second Octave - there is only half a step. Always imagine the octave as a sound "ladder" that has only seven steps - five whole steps and two half steps.

The seven main sounds of the octave: C, D, E, F, G, A and B differ from each other by the pitch of the step on which they stand. But musicians do not say "one step higher or lower", they say - "one TONE higher or lower". Therefore, it turns out that the sound D is higher than the sound C by one TONE, E is higher than D by one TONE, and the sound F is higher than the sound E only by HALF A TONE. G is higher than F by one TONE, A is higher than G by one TONE, B is also higher than A by one TONE. But the sound C of the second octave is higher than the sound B only by HALF A TONE.

1. Count how many tones are in an octave. It turns out that there are SIX TONES in total: five whole tones and two times half tones. And this means that the distance from the sound "C" of one octave to the sound "C" of the next octave is also equal to SIX TONES. Only musicians do not say - "the distance between sounds", they say - "INTERVAL between sounds". (The Latin word interval just means - "gap", "distance"). Therefore, it turns out that the interval of one octave is equal to six tones.

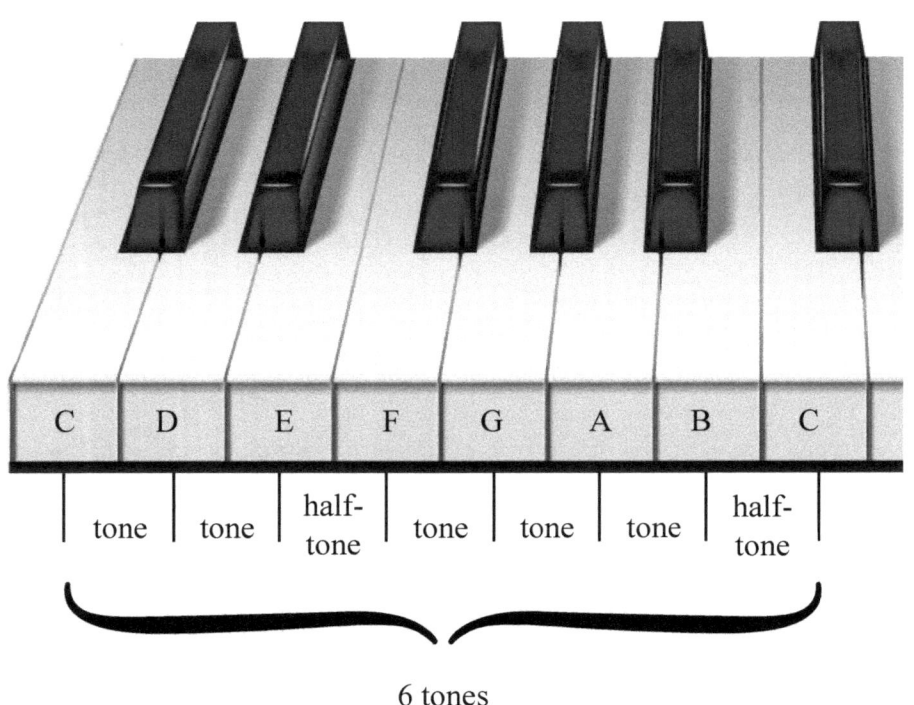

6 tones

**Remember!** An interval is a combination of two sounds taken one after the other in sequence or taken simultaneously. An interval is a very important musical concept, because any melody consists of an unbroken chain of intervals that arise when moving from one sound from one note to another. For example intervals form the sounds: C-D, C-E, E-G, etc.

# LEARN TO WRITE MUSICAL SOUNDS ON
# SHEET PAPER AND READ MUSIC

Musicians have learned to write down musical sounds on paper long ago.

To do this they turned the "sound ladder" into a flat "ladder" with five crossbars. And the main musical sounds began to be written down using oval circles directly on these crossbars and in the spaces between the crossbars.

1. Open a clean MUSIC NOTEBOOK. Musical sounds are written down using FIVE long lines. As soon as an oval circle falls on these lines, it begins to be called a "NOTE".

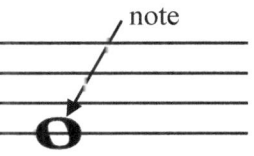

The Latin word "note" means "sign", "designation". Therefore, it turns out that a NOTE designates a musical sound of an octave and shows its position on the steps of the sound "ladder".

The five lines on which the notes are written are called by one common word - STAFF. Each line of the staff has its own ordinal number which is counted from the bottom up as in this picture. The five long lines of the staff are also called the main lines.

5 ———————————————————————————— FIFTH line ⎫
4 ———————————————————————————— FOURTH line ⎬ MAIN LINES
3 ———————————————————————————— THIRD line ⎪
2 ———————————————————————————— SECOND line ⎬
1 ———————————————————————————— FIRST line ⎭

Before writing down notes you need to learn how to draw a special sign called the Treble clef. The Treble clef "hangs" at the very beginning of the staff and "locks" the SECOND line so that it is immediately G visible that this line is occupied by the G note of the FIRST octave, as shown in the picture.

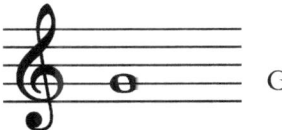

Learn to draw the Treble clef as shown in the picture. Outline the already drawn Treble clef.

Now draw the Treble clef at the very beginning of the clean staff. Step back to the right of the Treble clef and write the G note on the 2nd line. Above the G note, write two notes in order - A and B. Below the G note, write four notes in order - F, E, D and C. Then add the note C of the second octave. Everything should turn out as in this picture.

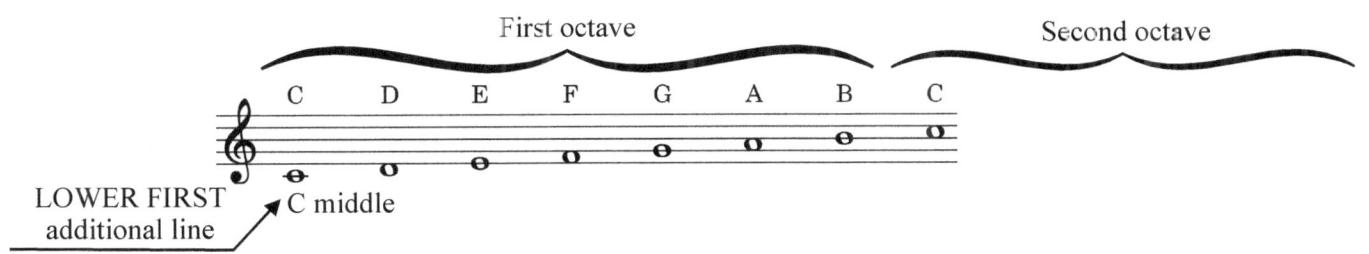

LOWER FIRST
additional line ⟋ C middle

13

To write the note C middle one more short line is added to the five main lines of the staff from below. It is called the lower first ADDITIONAL line.

Look at this staff and do not forget that wonderful transformation when the STEPS of the "staircase" with SOUNDS turned into LINES of the staff with NOTES.

2. And now let's connect together the staff on which the seven sounds of the FIRST octave and the sound C of the SECOND octave are written, and the eight keys of the piano which you need to press to play these sounds.

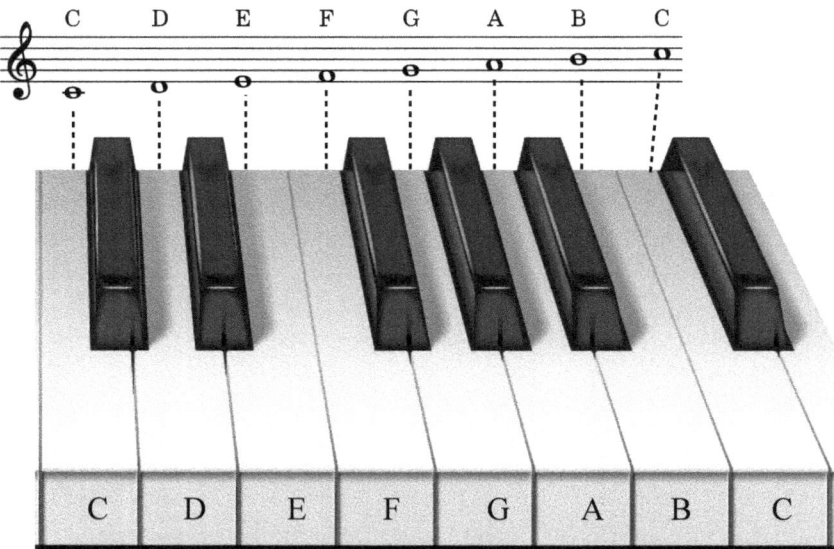

Look at this drawing every day and remember how the notes are arranged on the staff and the keys on the keyboard.

3. Now look at this drawing of your RIGHT hand.

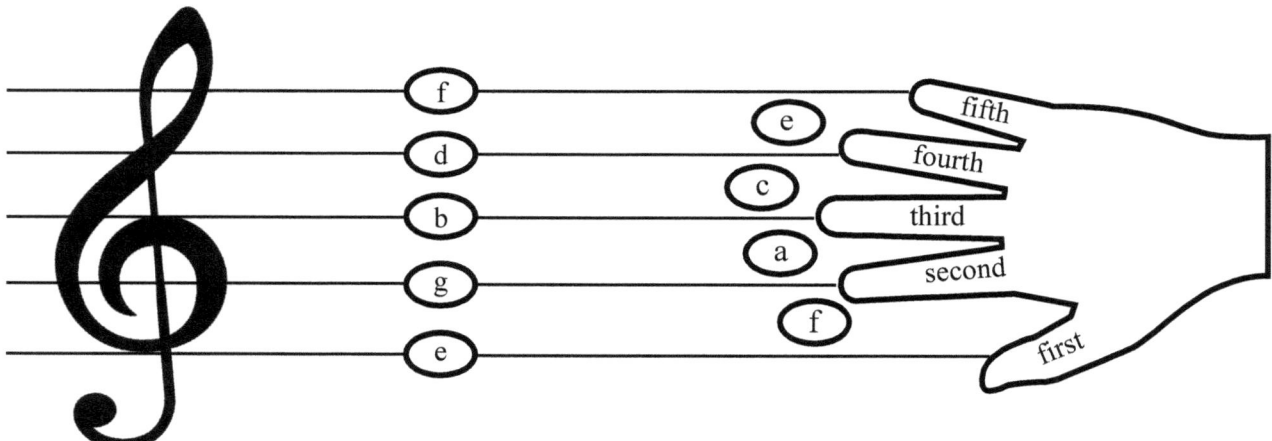

Imagine that the five fingers of your right hand are the five lines of the staff. Wherever you are: at home, at school or on the street, if you have a free minute, look at your right hand and remember how the notes are "arranged" on your fingers and between your fingers. The note G and the Treble clef "sit" on the 2nd finger.

14

# LEARN TO WRITE DOWN "LONG" AND "SHORT" SOUNDS AND PLAY "LONG" AND "SHORT" NOTES

Imagine that you are standing at a station and hear a train whistle: "Goo-oo-oo-oo!" This sound hangs in the air for a long time until the train leaves the station. It was a LONG sound, because it lasted and sounded for a long, long time.

Now imagine how the wheels of a tram "knock" on the rails: "Knock-knock! Tack-tack! Knock-knock! Tack-tack!" These sounds are SHORT, they "run" one after another, and each of them sounds for a very short time. In life, we are always surrounded by sounds of different lengths - long, drawn-out sounds and short, abrupt ones. In musical melodies, sounds of different lengths are also heard - both long and short. But musicians do not say - "length of sound", they say "DURATION of sound" or "DURATION of note". All musical sounds have not ONLY their own pitch. They also have their own specific duration. The duration of musical sounds is also written down using notes.

1. Press the C key, hold it down and count out loud evenly: "One, two, three, four!" After the word "four" release the key. The C note has now sounded for four counts or, as musicians say, it has sounded for FOUR FRACTIONS of time. **Remember!** *Counting out loud or in your mind, you count fractions of time.* A note whose duration is counted in four counts - "One, two, three, four!", and which sounds for four fractions of time, is called a WHOLE note. This is the "longest" note in music. Sounds of the greatest duration are written down in whole notes. A whole note looks like an oval circle, as in this picture.

2. Now you should learn how to count and play whole notes correctly.
The picture shows how to press the C and D keys correctly when playing whole notes.

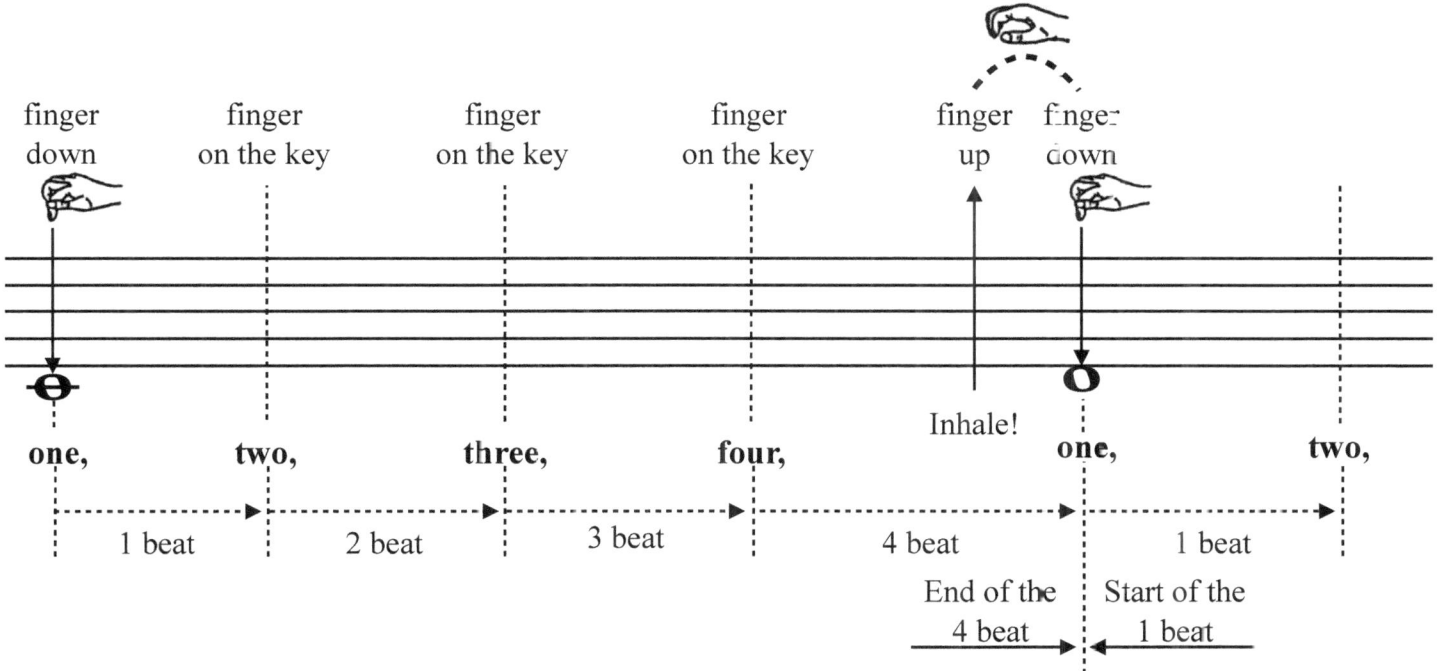

You say "one" and press your finger on the C key. You say "two," "three," and hold the key down. You say "four," take a small breath (if necessary), lift your finger off the C key, and move your hand smoothly to the D key. Then you say "one" again and press your finger on the D key.

The whole note C was now counted in four beats and sounded for four beats of time, as shown in the picture. The whole note D is counted and played in exactly the same way.

Pay attention to the most important thing: the end of the fourth beat of the note C exactly coincides with the beginning of the first beat of the note D. Therefore, so that your finger is not "late" to the D key, you must lift it from the C key a little earlier, without waiting for the end of the fourth beat. And then, simultaneously with the beginning of the first beat, on the count of "one", press the D key. In order for your playing to be smooth, you do not need to "pull" your finger off the key on the count of "four", but you need to smoothly remove it after this count - in the interval between the words "four" and "one". You must learn to do this well, because the beauty of the melodies that you will soon play will depend on the smooth transition from one note to another.

3. When you played whole notes, you certainly felt that these were very "long" notes. Therefore, in order to record "shorter" sounds, a whole note is divided in half into TWO equal parts. From one whole note you get TWO HALF notes as shown in this picture.

This is how you divide a WHOLE note into two HALF notes

And here is how HALF notes are depicted

Half notes also look like oval circles, but with a "stick" that "sticks out" up or down. The duration of a half note is equal to half the duration of a whole note. Therefore, a half note is counted in two: "One, two!", and sounds two beats of time - exactly half as long as a whole note.

Press the C key, hold it down and count out loud evenly: "One, two!" After the word "two", release the key. The C note sounded for two counts, or two beats of time.

4. Now you should learn how to count and play half notes correctly.

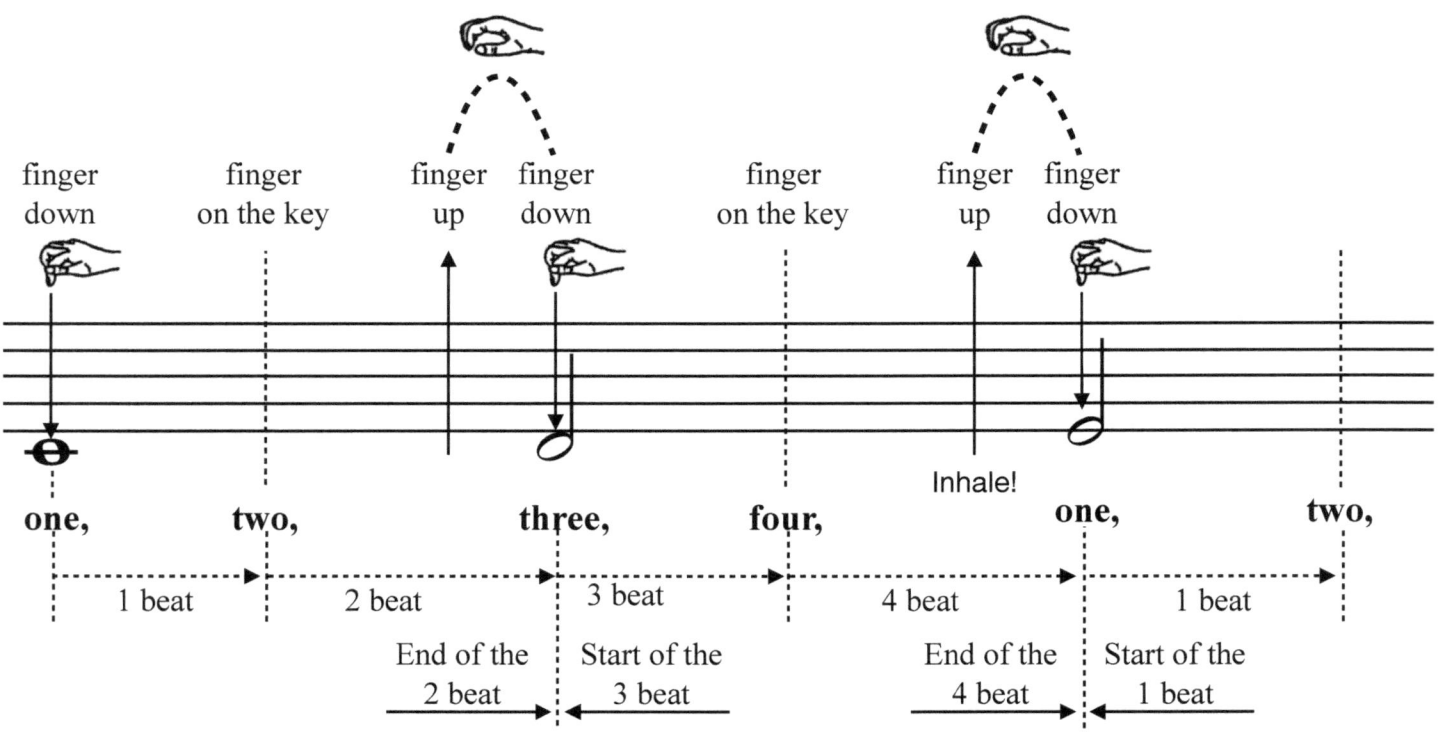

The picture shows how to press the keys C, D and E correctly when playing half notes.

You say "one" and press the C key. You say "two" and only then lift your finger from the C key and smoothly move your hand to the D key. You say "three" and press your finger on the D key. You say "four" and only then lift your finger from the D key and smoothly move your hand to the E key. Then you say "one" again and press the E key.

To make your playing smooth, you don't need to "pull" your finger off the C key on the count of "two", but rather smoothly remove it after this count - in the interval between the words "two" and "three".
Likewise, don't rush to remove your finger from the D key on the count of "four", but smoothly remove it after this count - in the interval between the word "four" and the second word "one". You should make these transitions from key to key smoothly and completely imperceptibly to the ear. And, of course, all these transitions must be done without straying from the even count.

5. When you played half notes, you certainly felt "by ear" that these were also "long" notes. Therefore, in order to record "short" sounds, a whole note is divided into FOUR equal parts. And then from one whole note you get four QUARTER notes, as shown in the picture.

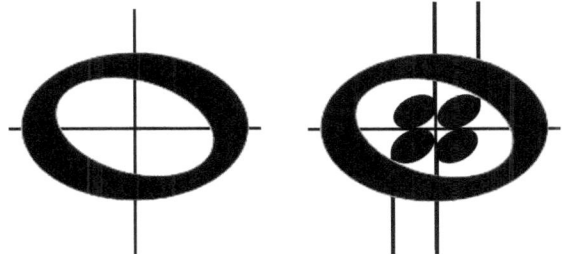

This is how a WHOLE note is
divided into four QUARTER notes

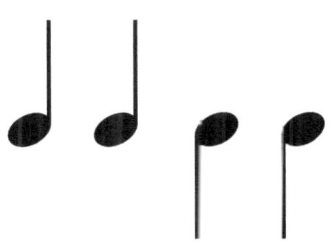

And here is how QUARTER
NOTES are depicted

Quarter notes also look like oval circles with "sticks", but these circles are black.

After this division, the duration of a quarter note is equal to one fourth of the duration of a whole note. And therefore, a quarter note is counted only for one count "One!" It lasts and sounds only for one fraction of the time - exactly four times less than a whole note. If you add up the durations of four quarter notes, you get two half notes or one whole note, as shown in the picture.

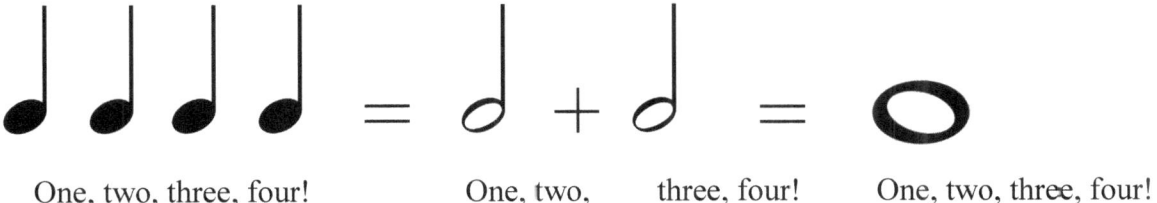

One, two, three, four!          One, two,     three, four!     One, two, three, four!

Very often a quarter note is called by one word - "quarter".

6. Now you should learn how to count and play quarter notes (quarters) correctly.

The picture shows how to press the keys C, D, E, F and G correctly when playing quarter notes.

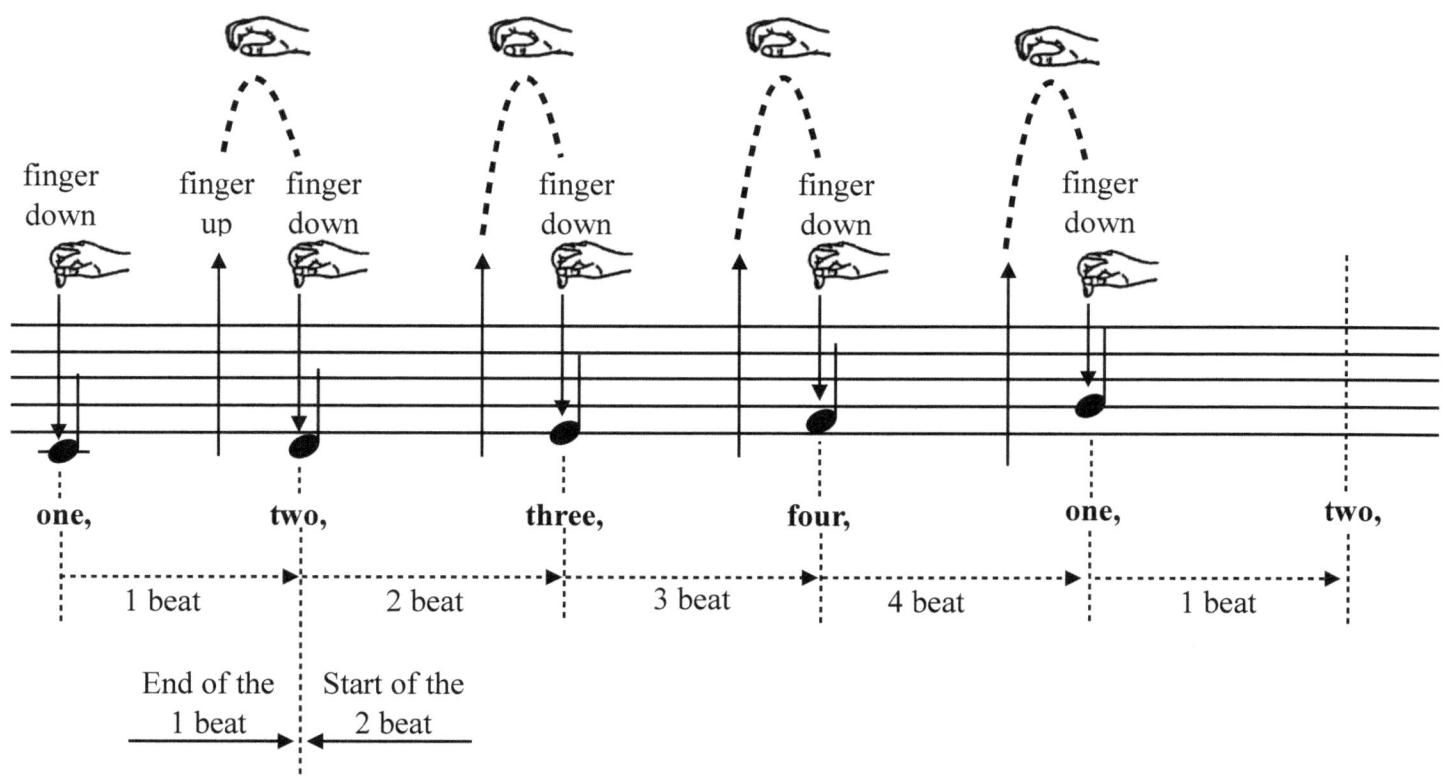

You say "one" and press your finger on the C key. Then lift your finger from the C key and smoothly move your hand to the D key. You say "two" and press the D key. Then lift your finger from the D key and smoothly move your hand to the E key. You say "three" and press the E key. You count and press the F and G keys in the same way.

Pay attention to the most important thing: the END of the duration of each note (time fraction) exactly coincides with the BEGINNING of the duration of the next note. Therefore, so that your finger does not "float" from one key to another, you must lift it from the keys a little earlier, without waiting for the full end of the duration (time fraction) of each note. And then, on each successive count, simultaneously with the beginning of the new beat, press the next keys. This transition from note to note must be SMOOTH, unhurried and completely imperceptible to the ear. And, of course, this transition must be made without straying from the UNIFORM count for a single moment. The hand and finger must be moved from key to key very smoothly. Otherwise, the melody that you will play will definitely be "limping", and the notes and sounds will "stutter". The shorter the notes and sounds, the more audible "by ear" all your inaccuracies and irregularities. Remember and follow the main rule: count QUARTERS evenly and SMOOTHLY move your hand and fingers.

# UNDERSTAND HOW A MUSICAL MELODY IS "ORGANISED"

When a beautiful song is sung, it immediately seems that there is a great similarity between its melody and the lyrics. And so it is. The fact is that the poem and the musical melody are "arranged" in a very similar way. The poem, like "bricks", is built from words. And the melody, like "bricks", is built from musical sounds. Let's figure out what the "bricks" of the poem and the "bricks" of the musical melody have in common.

1. Read aloud with expression four lines from the poem. Those words that "ask" to be emphasised by the voice and pronounced with more force and emphasis are marked with special signs.> - this is the STRESS sign. It is also called the ACCENT sign.

> With a rosy dawn
> The east was covered.
> In the village beyond the river
> The light went out.

Write these verses in one line, but separate each line from the other with a vertical line. You should get four of these "bricks".

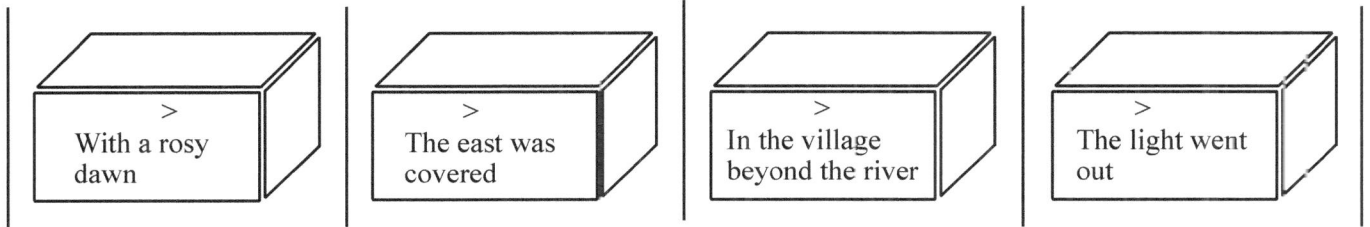

In each "brick" replace the words of the poem with the count "One, two!" This is what you get.

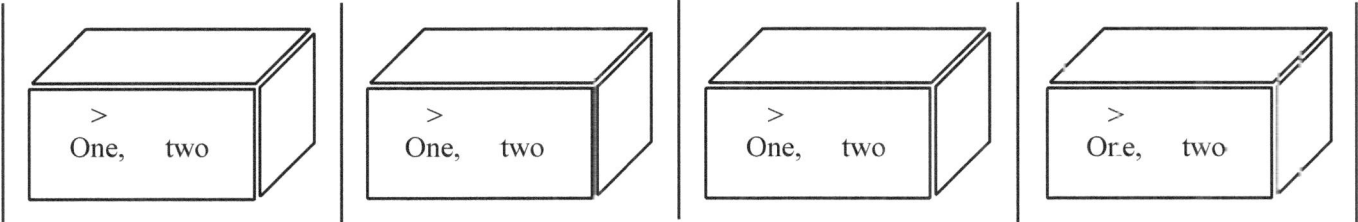

In front of you are four identical "bricks". Each of them consists of two SHARE, which are counted in two counts: "One, two!" The first beat is stressed, accented.

Musical melodies are also built from very similar "bricks". In music, these "bricks" are called MEASURES. When notes are written on a staff one measure is separated from another by a vertical line which is called a MEASURE LINE. A measure that consists of TWO beats is called a TWO-BEAT.

Two-beat measure

Bar line                                    Bar line

One, two!

A duple measure is counted in two: "One, two." The first beat of the measure is called the STRONG, or HEAVY, beat, because it is the one on which the accent falls. The second beat is called the WEAK, or LIGHT, beat.

2. Two duple measures can be joined together to form one COMPLEX, quadruple measure, as shown in this picture.

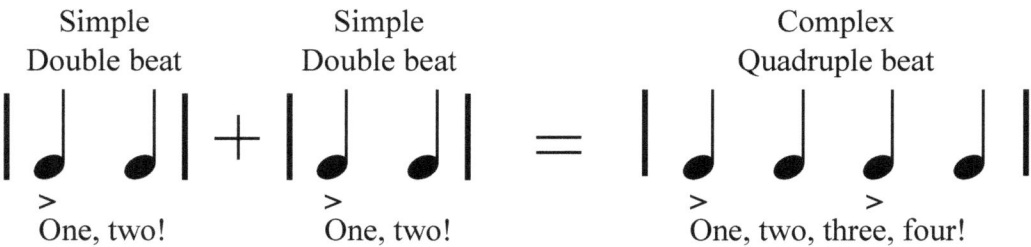

A four-beat measure consists of FOUR beats and is counted in FOUR counts: "One, two, three, four!" This measure has TWO ACCENTS and TWO STRONG beats - the first and the third.
But only the third beat is weaker than the first. But the second and fourth beats in this measure are WEAK, because they were weak in their two-beat measures.

3. If a measure consists of THREE beats, it is called a TRIPLE-BEAT and is counted in THREE counts, as shown in the picture.

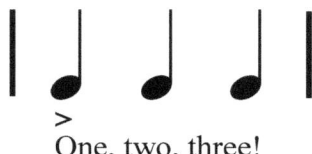

This is a SIMPLE measure because it has only one accent on the first strong beat. The second and third beats in this measure are weak.

Pay attention: the FIRST beat in each measure is STRONG, because it has an ACCENT. It turns out that the measure line is put in the notes in order to constantly indicate where in the musical melody the strong beats are and where accents (stresses) should be made.

# CHAPTER II

## LEARN TO PLAY PIECES

In music, the word "Piece" can mean many things. A song, a dance, or a musical melody are all called a piece if they are specifically written for an instrument.

## THE FIRST THREE PIECES FOR ONE FINGER OF ONE HAND

Play each piece in turn with the 3rd and 2nd fingers of your right hand, then with the 3rd and 2nd fingers of your left hand.

### 1. SPARROW

**Moderately**

Arranged by J. Mercer

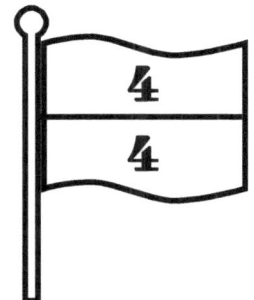

This piece, which is best played with a teacher, has four measures. The measures are counted in order from left to right, starting from the Treble clef. At the end of the last measure there is a double line - ‖. In the notes this line marks the end of the piece.

Immediately after the Treble clef on the staff there are the two numbers 𝄴. These two numbers are called the SIZE OF THE MEASURE. They stand on the staff like a road sign stands on the road. The size of the measure indicates in what groups the notes "march" on the staff and how they should be counted. The upper number "**4**" says that these are quadruple measures. This means that they consist of FOUR beats and are counted in four counts. The lower number "4" says that each beat of the measure is one QUARTER note, which is counted in one count - "one". It is clear that a measure of this size can "fit" four QUARTER notes or two HALF notes, or one WHOLE note. The size of the measure 𝄴 is read and pronounced - "four quarters".

Above the staff there is an indication - "Moderately". This is an indication of the speed with which you need to count the measures. The speed of your playing depends on the speed of counting. But musicians usually say the "TEMPO" of playing instead of the word "speed". It turns out that you should count and play this piece at a moderate speed, at a calm tempo.

## 2. THE GAME

Arranged by J. Mercer

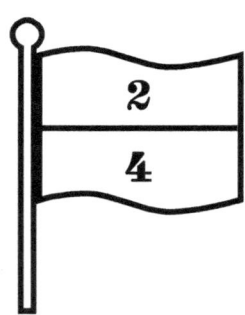

In this piece the SIZE of the measures is indicated by numbers: $\frac{2}{4}$. The upper number "**2**" says that these are TWO-BEAT measures. This means that they consist of TWO beats and are counted on two counts. The lower number "**4**" says that each beat of the measure is one QUARTER note which is counted on one count - "one". This means that a measure of this size can fit two QUARTER notes or one HALF note. The measure size of $\frac{2}{4}$ is read and pronounced - "two quarters".

Note: just as the dial of a clock is divided by numbers and dashes into equal intervals of time so the measure line also divides the staff into equal parts of time.

## 3. THE TRAIN PASSES BY

Arranged by J. Mercer

Before playing this piece imagine that you are standing at a station. A train approaches and blows its whistle from afar. The train gradually approaches closer and closer but does not stop, quickly passes by, and gradually disappears into the distance.

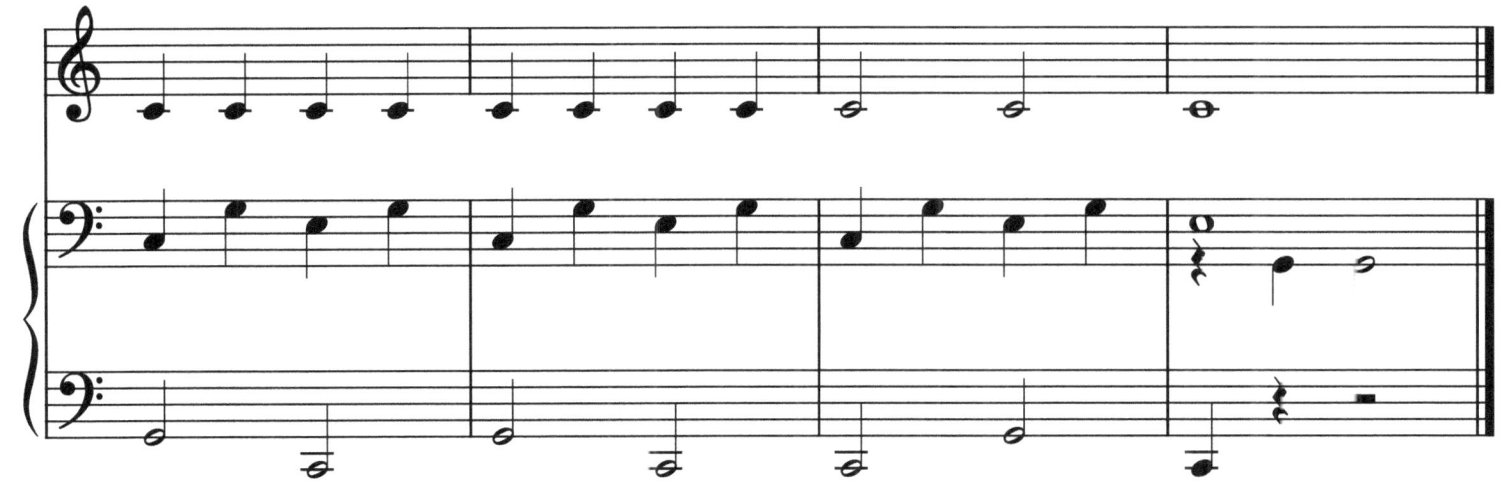

## FIVE PIECES FOR ONE HAND

Play these pieces first with your right hand, then with your left hand. The numbers *above the staff* indicate the numbers of the fingers of your right hand that you need to press the keys with when playing the piece. The numbers *below the staff* indicate the numbers of the fingers for your left hand.

**Remember!** The order of alternating fingers and its designation with numbers in the notes is called - FINGERING.

When playing the pieces, you will first press the keys with only the 2nd and 3rd fingers. Then the 4th finger will join the 2nd and 3rd, and later - the 1st and 5th.

The first fingers, unlike the other four, press the keys not with their tips - "pads", but with their side surfaces. The pictures show how you will press the keys with the first fingers of your right and left hands.

### 4. THE SUN IN THE WINDOW

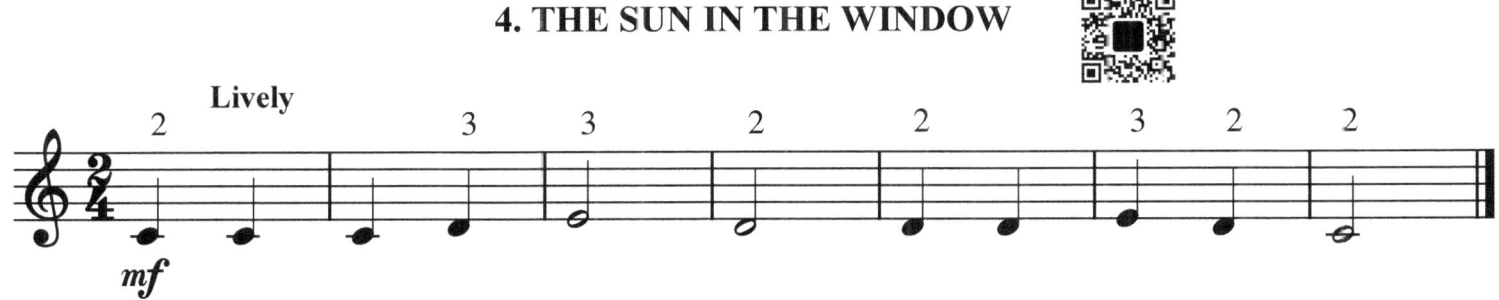

# LEARN TO PLAY WITH TWO HANDS THREE PIECES FOR ONE FINGER OF EACH HAND

## 9. THE WATCH

Arranged by J. Mercer

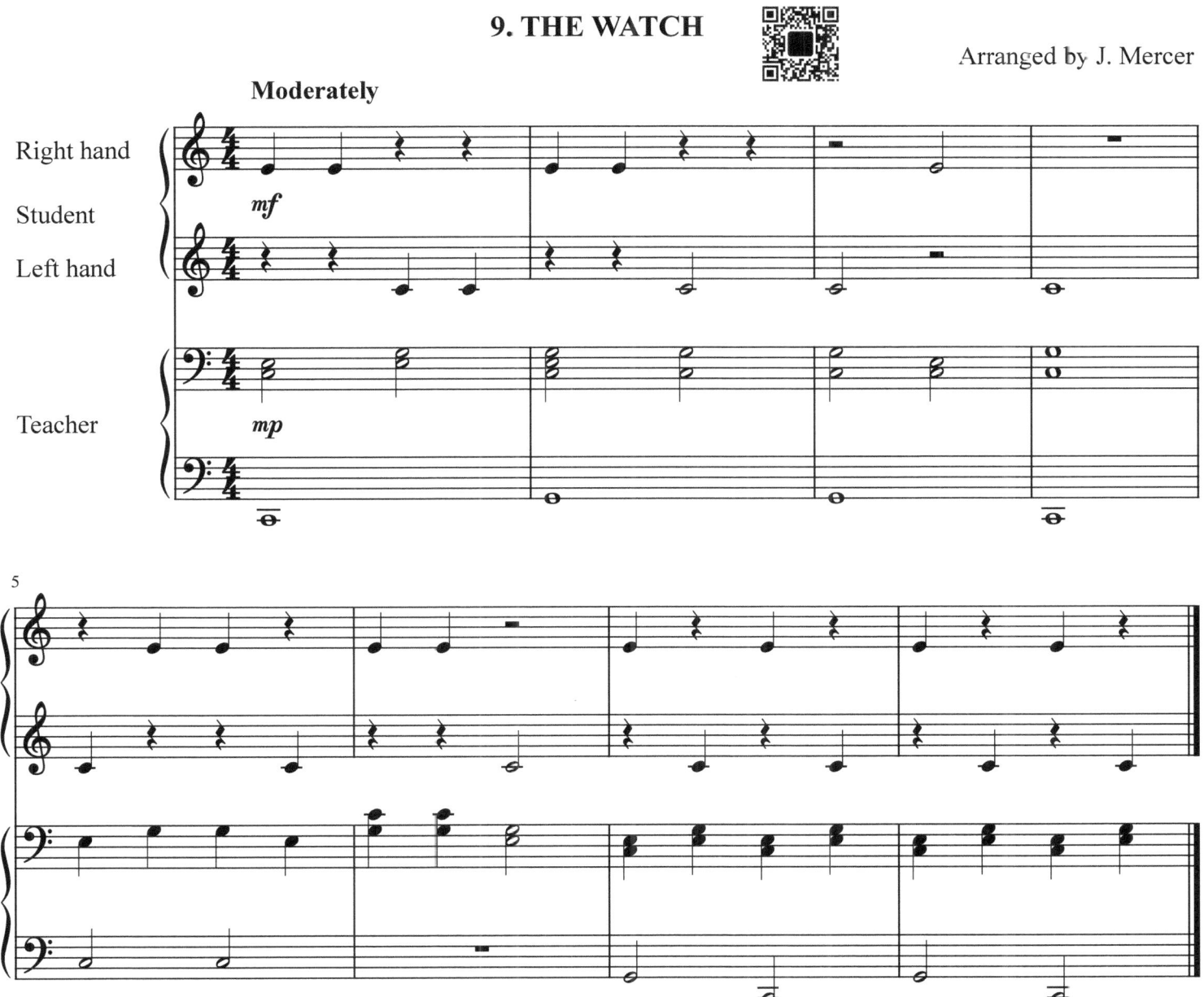

This piece is written on two staves at once - the upper and lower. On the UPPER staff the notes for the RIGHT hand are written and on the LOWER - for the LEFT. Both staves are united by a common vertical line and a curly bracket which is called ACCOLADE. This French word means "unification". At the very end of both staves there is a common DOUBLE vertical line. This line marks the END of the piece.

In each measure you see new signs on the upper and lower staves: ♦ and ▬. In the 3rd, 4th and 6th measures, they look like a road sign "No entry" as in this picture. These new signs are called PAUSES and also prohibit playing in the place of the staff where they are. The pause sign means that the sound of the notes is interrupted and there is a BREAK in the melody. The rest is not played, but counted out loud or in the mind exactly as if it were a note. Therefore rests have the same duration as regular notes. Rests are indicated by special signs, which are shown in this figure.

25

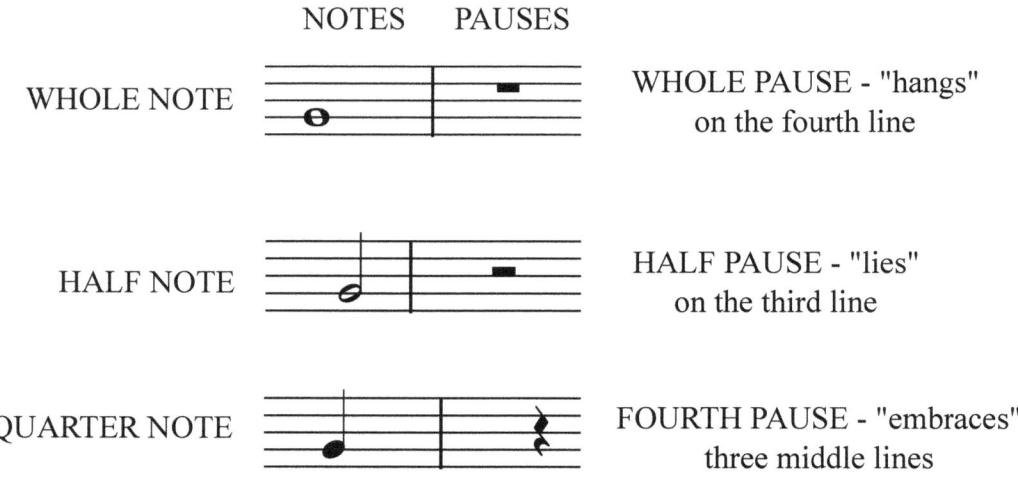

| NOTES | PAUSES |
|---|---|

WHOLE NOTE — WHOLE PAUSE - "hangs" on the fourth line

HALF NOTE — HALF PAUSE - "lies" on the third line

QUARTER NOTE — FOURTH PAUSE - "embraces" three middle lines

It is best if you imagine that the pause is a SILENT note. It demands to be COUNTED but it itself is SILENT.

Play the piece with one finger of the right and one finger of the left hand, alternately: 3rd and 2nd.
Finally, play with the 2nd finger of the right hand and the 3rd finger of the left. And then vice versa: with the 3rd finger of the right hand and the 2nd finger of the left.

# 10. AFTER THE RAIN

Arranged by J. Mercer

26

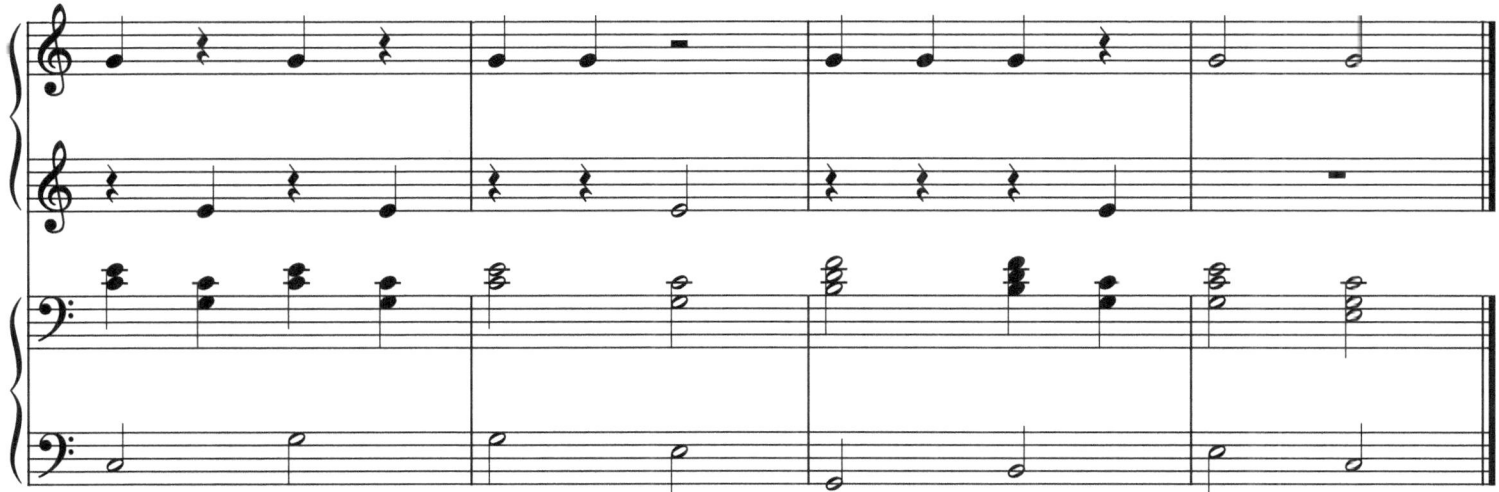

Play the piece with one finger of the right hand and one finger of the left: 3rd and 2nd. Finally, play with the 2nd finger of the right hand and the 3rd finger of the left. And then vice versa: with the 3rd finger of the right hand and the 2nd finger of the left.

Play the next piece, "The Dove", in exactly the same way.

## 11. DOVE

**Moderately**

Arranged by J. Mercer

Student

Teacher

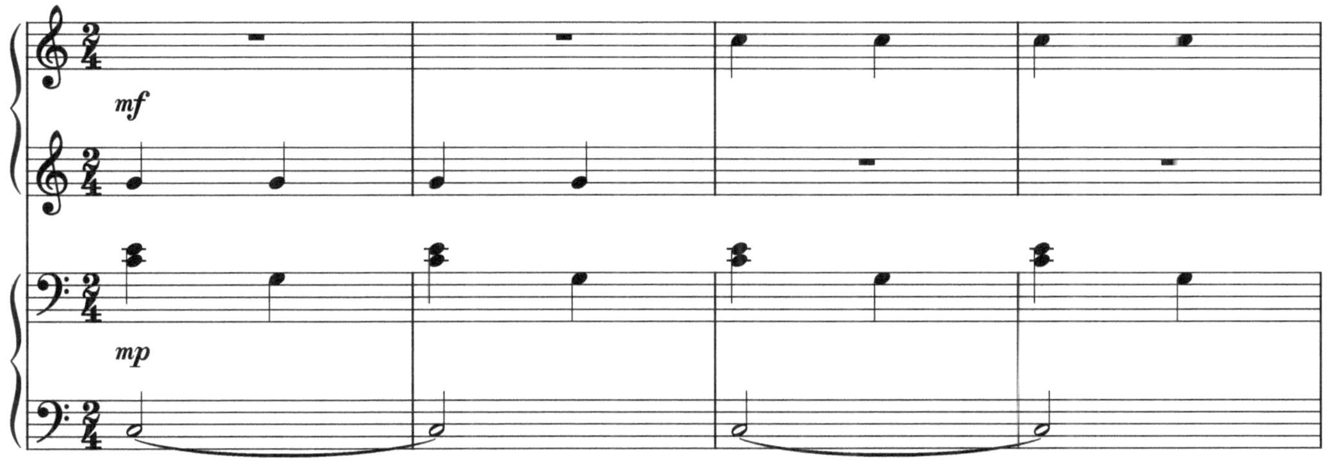


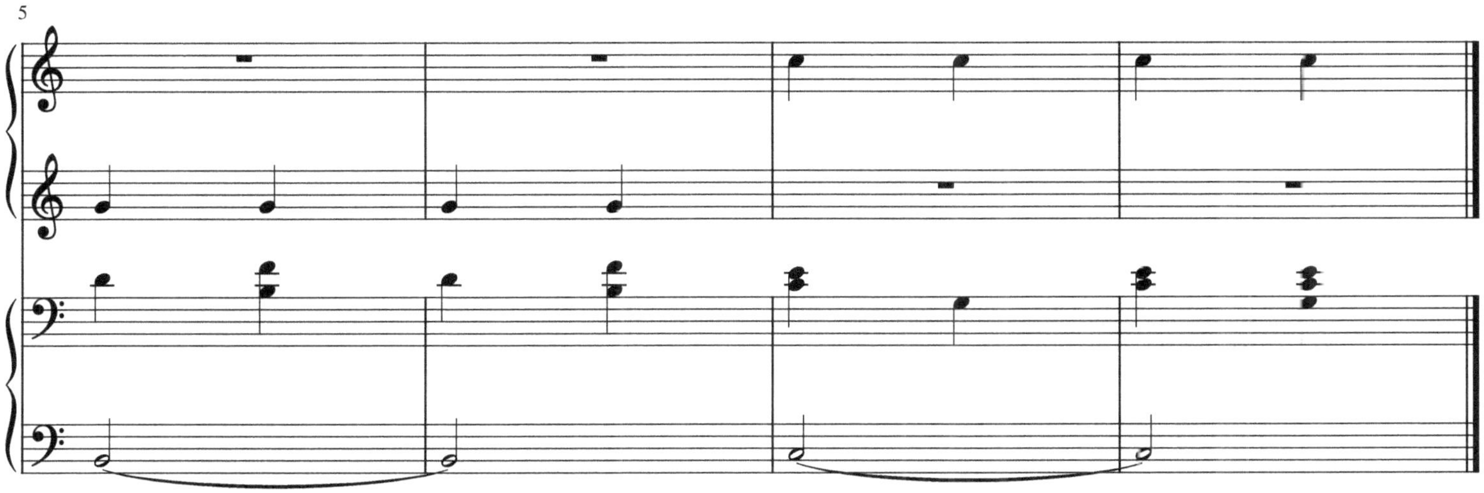

# SIX PIECES FOR TWO AND THREE FINGERS OF EACH HAND

## 12. CHRISTMAS TREE
### German song

Arranged by J. Mercer

Student

Teacher

If the tempo is marked as "Fun", you need to play a little faster than at a MODERATE tempo and a little louder than MEDIUM volume. After all no one has fun quietly and barely moving their feet.

# KEEP PLAYING PIECES AND LEARN TO PLAY COHERENTLY

### 13. DREAM
### American Song

Arranged by J. Mercer

In this piece, the notes of the 1st, 2nd, 3rd, 5th, 6th and 7th measures are connected by an arc - ⌣. This arc is called - TIE. The notes that are connected by the tie sign must be played COHERENTLY. Before, you pressed the keys so that the sound of one note was clearly SEPARATED from the sound of the next note. You lifted your finger from the key, and only then lowered the other finger and pressed the next key. This way of playing the piano is called NON LEGATO. Now you must learn to play the second way, which is called LEGATO "coherently". In this way, the sound of one note smoothly and imperceptibly to the ear TRANSITIONS into the sound of the next note. One sound smoothly "flows" into another, they are inextricably linked with each other and the melody flows like water in a stream.

Before playing this piece do a useful exercise.

Curve the fingers of your right hand and hold them over the closed lid of the piano the way you usually hold your fingers over the keys. Press your fingertips on the surface of the lid and smoothly "step" from one finger to another: from the 2nd to the 3rd, from the 3rd to the 4th, from the 4th back to the 3rd, and from the 3rd to the 2nd. Lift your finger from the lid only when the next finger has already begun to "step" on the surface of the lid. Try to make these two moments coincide for you - one finger rises from the lid, but at the same moment the other finger already begins to press on the lid. Train the fingers of your right hand, then your left hand, until they start to "step over" EASILY and SMOOTHLY.

Now you can play the song "Dream" in the LEGATO manner.

Press the C key with the 3rd finger of your left hand. Without raising your hand up, "step over" the 2nd finger to the adjacent D key. Press D even before you completely release the C key. As soon as the 2nd finger completely "steps over" D, and you already begin to hear this sound, immediately remove the 3rd finger from the C key. Your two fingers should "tie" the second D sound to the C sound.

The hand seems to "step over" from finger to finger and from one key to another. Pay attention to the main thing: the fingers "step over", but the hand DOES NOT RISE above the keys. And in general, when playing *legato*, do not make sudden movements or pushes with your hand, and never raise your fingers too high. Try not only not to hit the keys with your fingers, but even the opposite - press the keys with a soft, slightly sliding motion, as if you were wiping dust off the key. Therefore, when playing *legato*, the fingers must move only in their upper joints.

**When playing legato only the upper joints move**

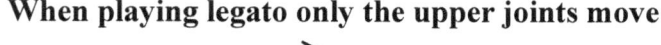
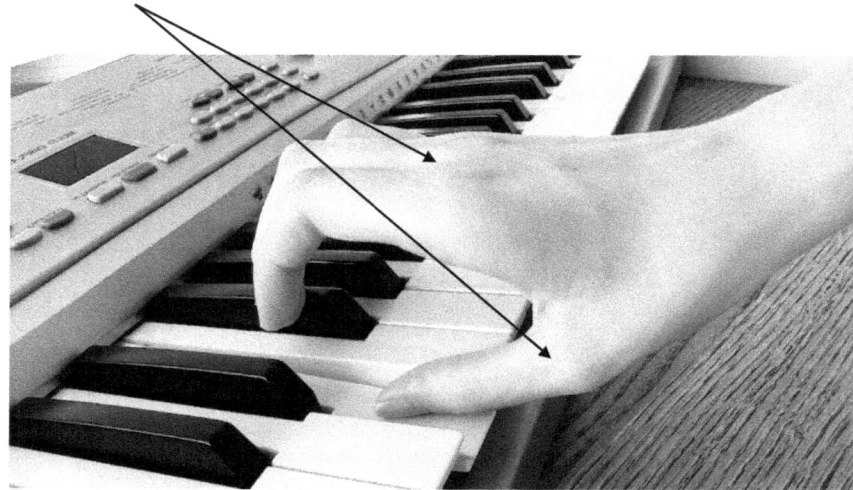

Play this piece as many times as you can until you get good at *legato*. Count out loud but be sure to listen to how one sound follows another and mentally imagine how each subsequent note will sound. Musicians call this "keeping your ear one note ahead of your fingers." Then your playing will become truly fluid and your piano keys will "sing".

# 14. MARY HAD A LITTLE LAMB
## American song

Arranged by J. Mercer

**Student**

**Teacher**

## 15. FASHIONABLE BUNNY
### French folk song

Arranged by J. Mercer

**Moderately**

Student

*mf*

Teacher

*mp*

32

# 16. SUNDAY
## German song

Arranged by J. Mercer

33

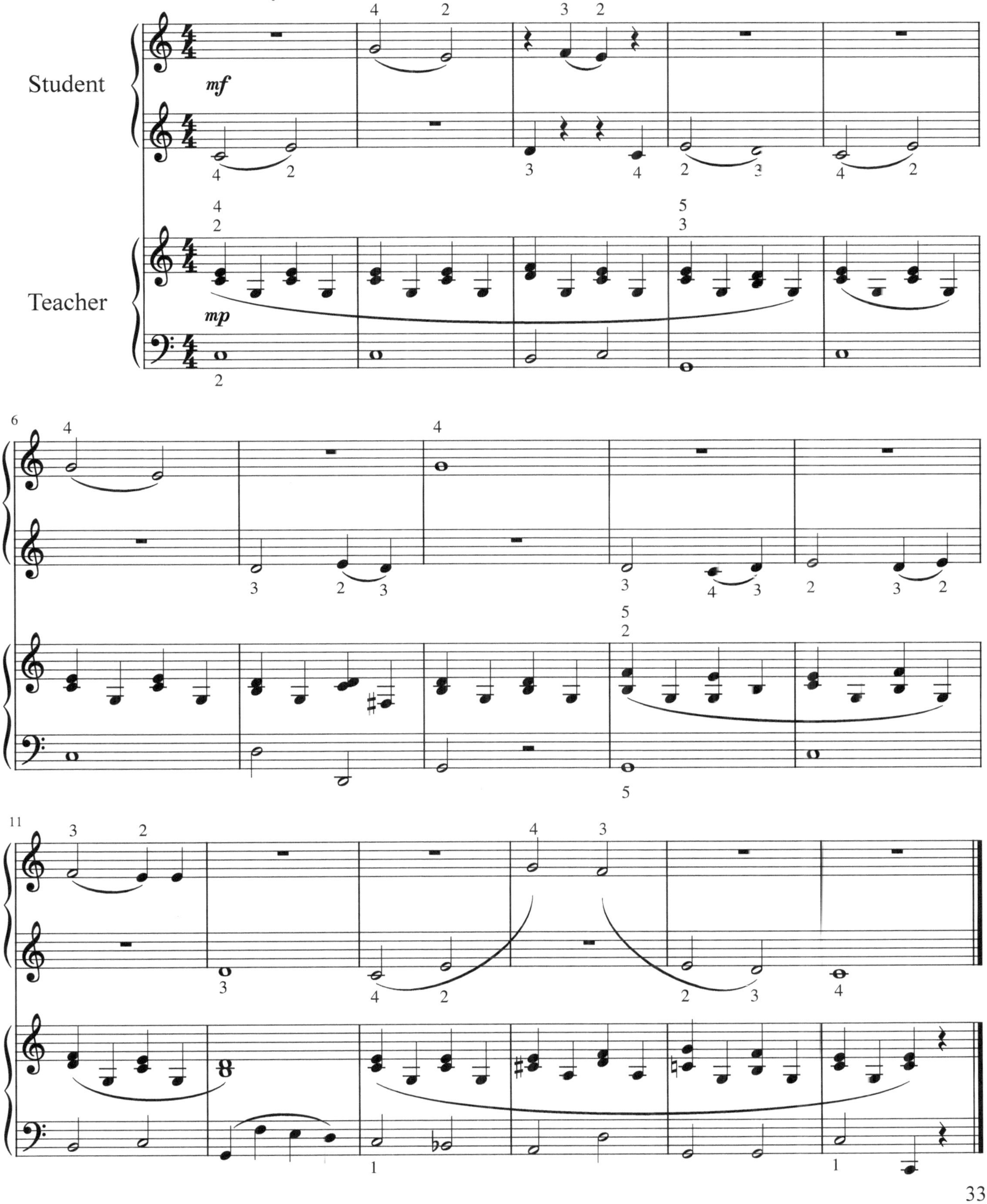

# 17. IN THE EVENING
## On the theme of a German school song

Arranged by J. Mercer

**Moderately**

Student

Teacher

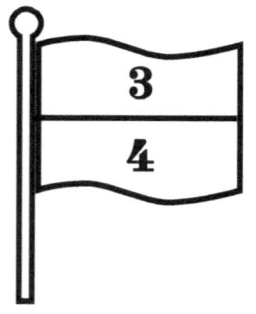

In this piece the SIZE of the measure is indicated by numbers: $\frac{3}{4}$. The upper number "3" says that the measures consist of THREE beats and they should be counted in three. counts: "One, two, three!" The lower number "4" says that each beat of the measure is one QUARTER note, which is counted in one count - "one". And this means that in a measure of this size there can be three QUARTER notes or one HALF and one QUARTER note together.

The measure size " $\frac{3}{4}$ " is read and pronounced - "three quarters". It turns out that the upper number says: "Count in three counts - one, two, three!"

And the lower number says: "Every one count is a quarter note".

# FIVE PIECES FOR FOUR AND FIVE FINGERS OF EACH HAND

## 18. FOR EXERCISES
### German song

Arranged by J. Mercer

## 19. KITTEN

Arranged by J. Mercer

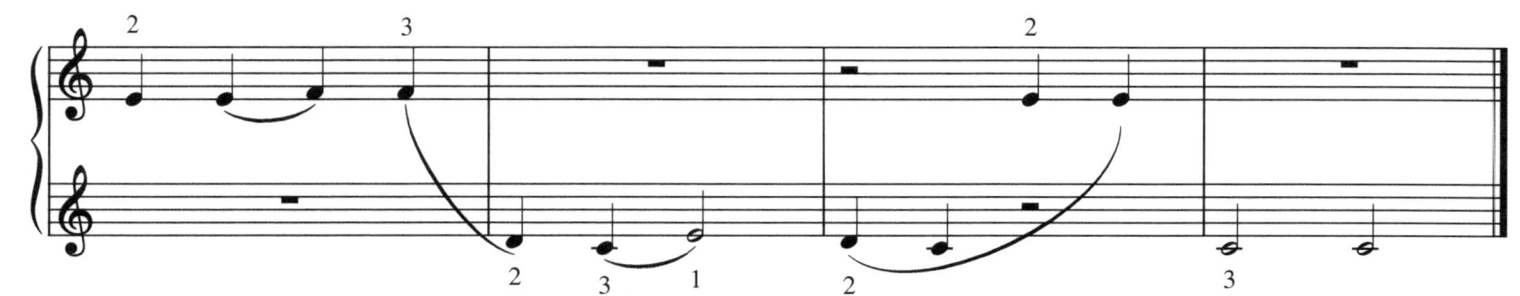

## 20. POLLY WOLLY DOODLE
### American Song

Arranged by J. Mercer

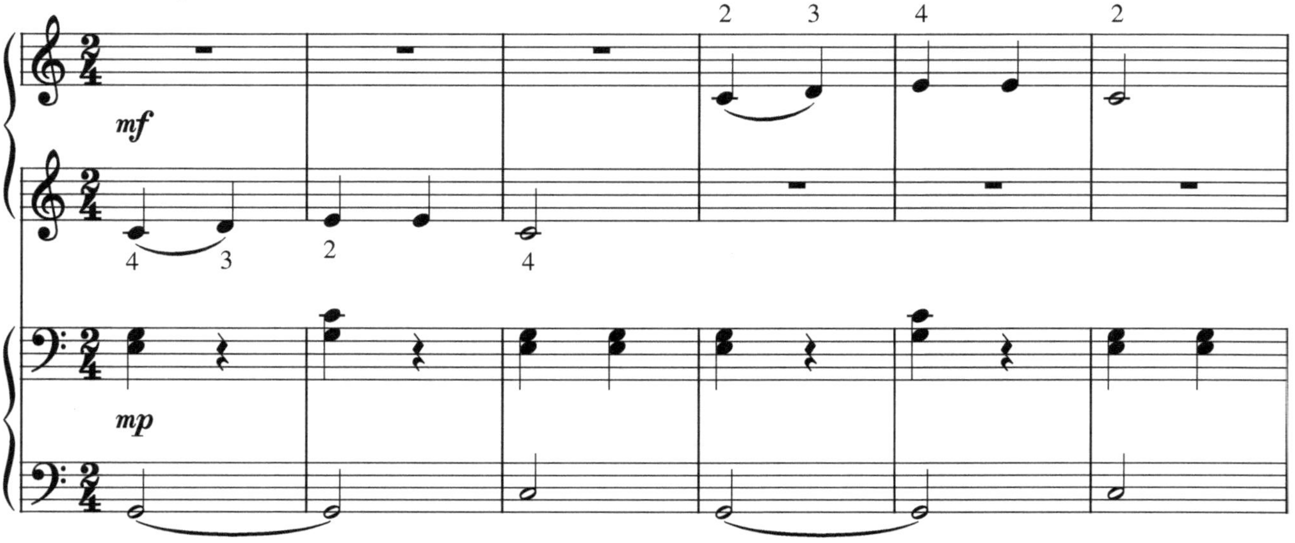

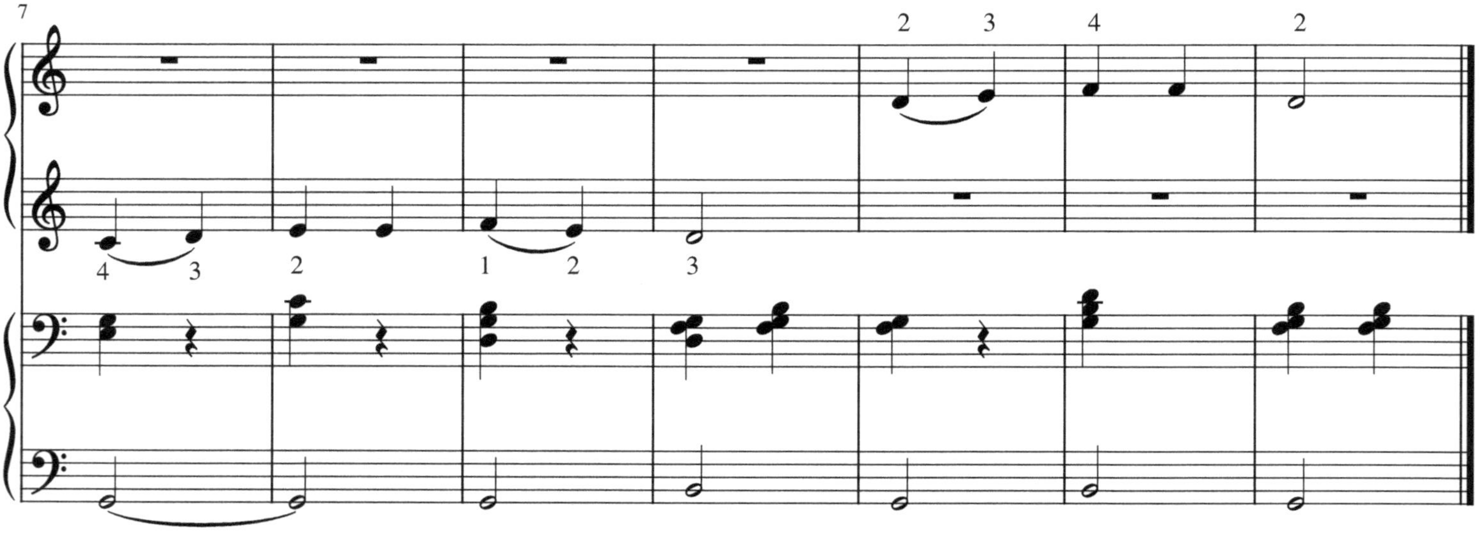

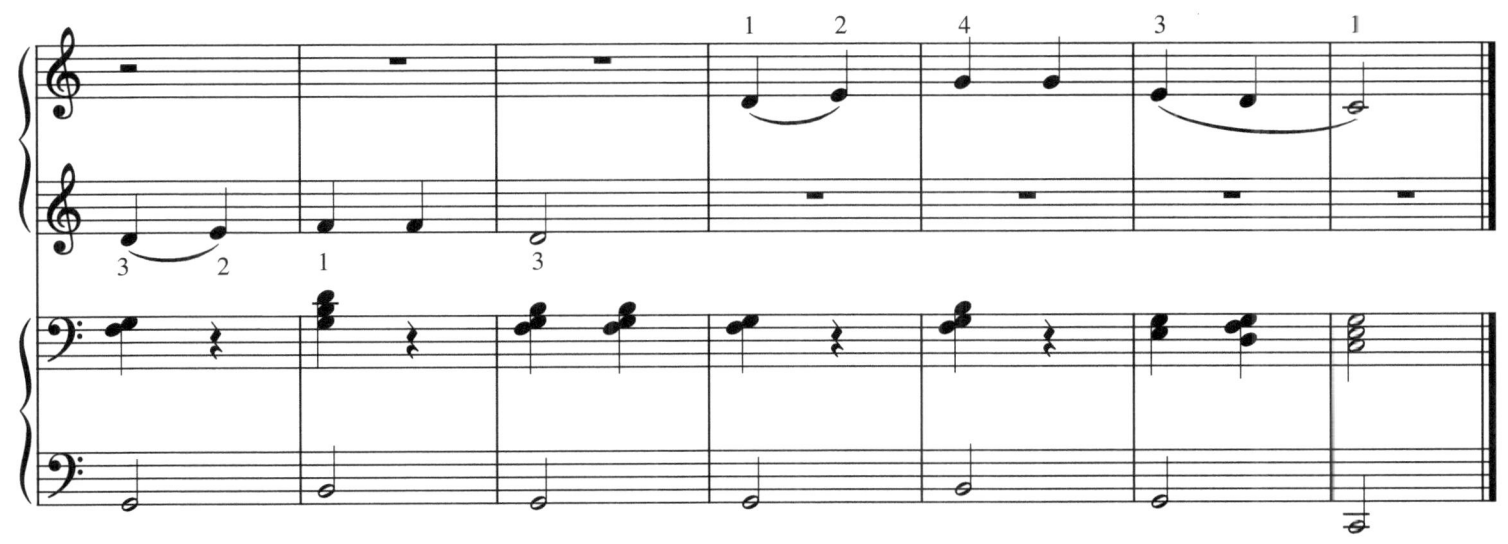

Finally, try playing this piece an octave higher for the right hand.

## 21. QUIET VALLEYS

Arranged by J. Mercer

**Calmly**

# 22. FIRST WALTZ
## On the theme of the English ballad "Your Eyes"

Arranged by J. Mercer

**In waltz tempo**

Student

Teacher

# FIRST PIECES IN THE TREBLE CLEF WITH "SAME" NOTES FOR BOTH HANDS

On this staff are written seven notes of the FIRST octave, seven notes of the SECOND octave and one more note C of the THIRD octave.

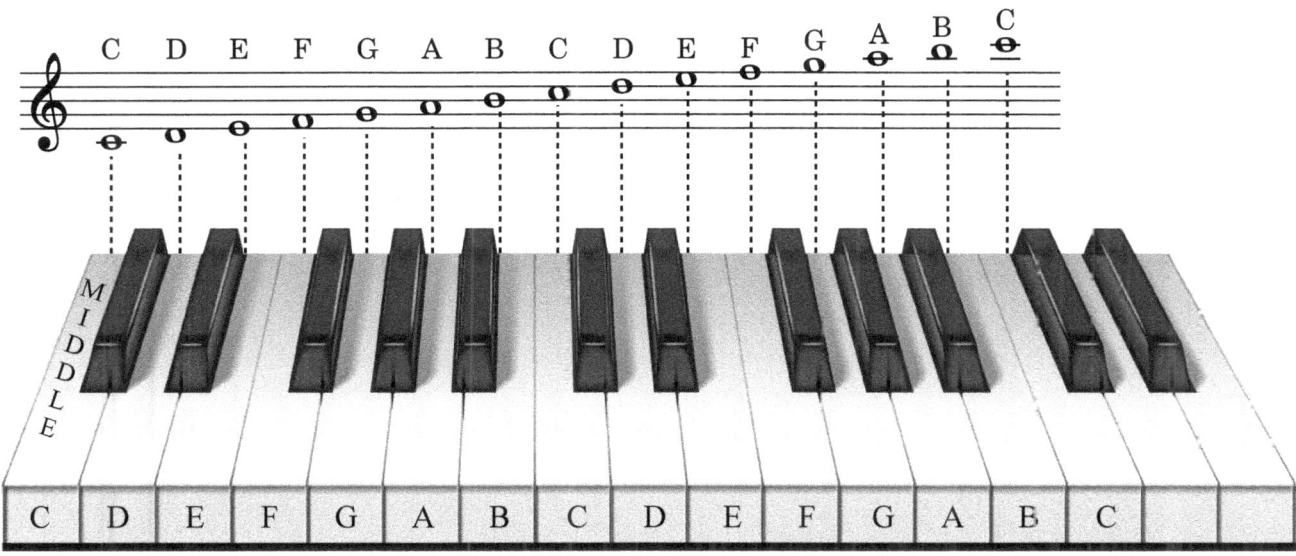

Remember how the keys of the second octave are located on the keyboard and the notes of the second octave on the staff.

To play computer games well, you need to quickly find the desired targets on the screen. To play the piano well, you need to quickly find the desired notes with your eyes.

This picture shows four lines of quarter notes. Pay attention to how they are written: if a note is BELOW the third line, then its "stick" is raised UP. If it is on the third line or ABOVE, then its "stick" is lowered DOWN.

Move your eyes from left to right along these lines and mentally determine which note is on the LINE and which is in the GAP. Do not call the notes by their names. "Walk" your eyes this way three times. The second and third times, try to "walk" the lines faster.

"Walk" the lines three more times, but now mentally determine on which COUNT line and in which COUNT gap the note is.

Now "walk" your eyes along the lines three times and mentally pronounce the NAMES of only those notes that are on the LINES. Do it faster each time.

"Walk" your eyes along the lines three times and mentally pronounce the NAMES of only those notes that are in the SPACES between the lines. Do this faster each time.

Now "go" over the lines three times, and mentally pronounce the names of all the notes IN A ROW - on the LINES and in the GAPS. Try to do it faster each time.

Sit at the piano and put these four lines of notes in front of you. With the second finger of your right hand, press the keys in order and loudly say "by name" each note. "Go" over the notes with your eyes and the keys with your finger five times. Try to do it faster each time.

Practice this before each lesson until you begin, almost without thinking, to name all the notes "by name" and press the necessary keys.

At first, you will play in the first and second octaves, which means - on the right side of the keyboard. Therefore, temporarily move your chair five white keys to the right. Check again whether you have chosen the right height of the chair. The main thing is that this height is such that you are comfortable sitting at the piano, and your hands automatically take a horizontal position when playing. Do not press your hands and elbows to your body when playing, but do not "let them go" too far either.

When reading notes and playing, you should not lean forward too much and "fall" onto the keyboard.

Try to change the chosen height of the chair and its distance from the keyboard as little as possible. Do not do this "for nothing better to do" or without special need.

Curl the fingers of both hands, as if they were "holding" glass balls, and move your hands to the keyboard, as shown in the picture.

**ROUND IT UP!**

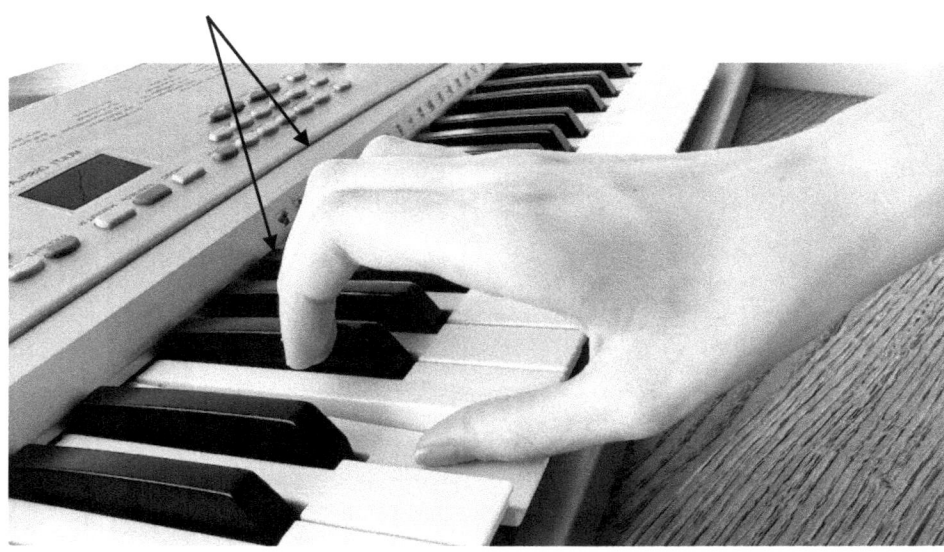

Distribute all ten fingers over the ten white keys as in this picture. With soft fingertips, lightly touch the keys.

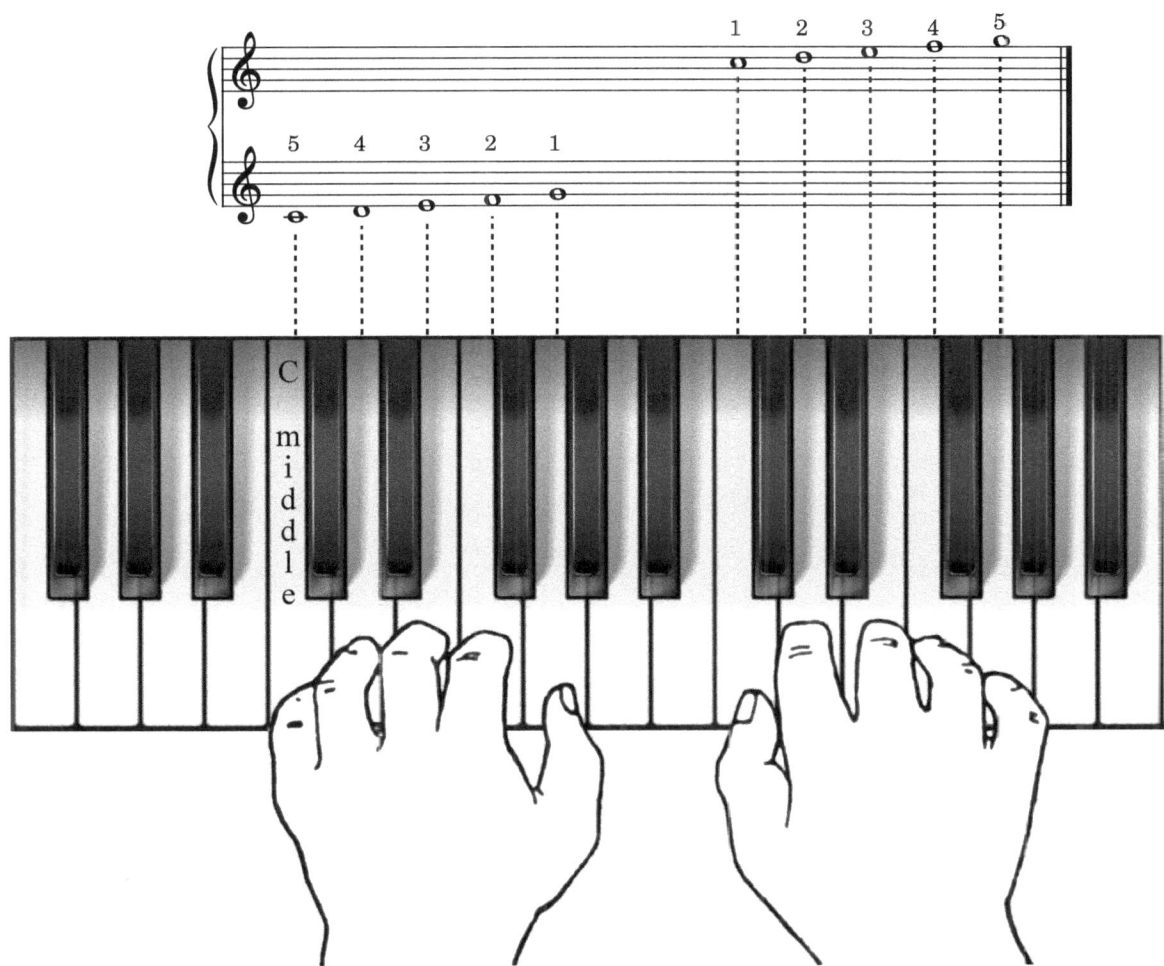

Let the 5th finger of the left hand touch the C key of the first octave (middle C), and the 1st finger of the right hand touch the C key of the second octave. Make sure that the hands and arms from the wrist to the elbow are at the same level. In other words, hold your hands so that the wrist is in line with the forearm. After rounding the fingers, their joints should not stick out and protrude - the fingers should have a natural rounded shape. Do not tense the hands and hold them loosely. Therefore, do not bend and round the fingers too much.

The 1st fingers should be slightly bent so that they are approximately in the same direction as the 5th fingers. Then their joints will be directed outward. Hold the hands loosely, without tension, and then they themselves will choose a comfortable position for themselves with a slight tilt towards the 5th finger. However, make sure that this tilt is not too great, because the 4th and 5th fingers must have sufficient range and freedom of movement when playing. Press the keys with the very tips - the soft "pads" of the rounded fingers. Only the 1st fingers can press and hit the keys with their outer side. Be especially careful that the 5th finger also presses the key with its tip, and not with its side.

There are NUMBERS on the upper and lower staff. These are the fingering numbers - the fingering for your RIGHT AND LEFT hands. You must play the corresponding.

All your ten fingers are distributed in a certain way over the ten keys. But musicians do not say: "The fingers are distributed", they say: "The fingers are in position".

Play new pieces in this "ten-finger" position. Pay special attention to the correct position of the hand and fingers. Do not allow the hand to "fall" towards the 1st or 5th fingers.

## 23. FROM FINGER TO FINGER

**Slowly**

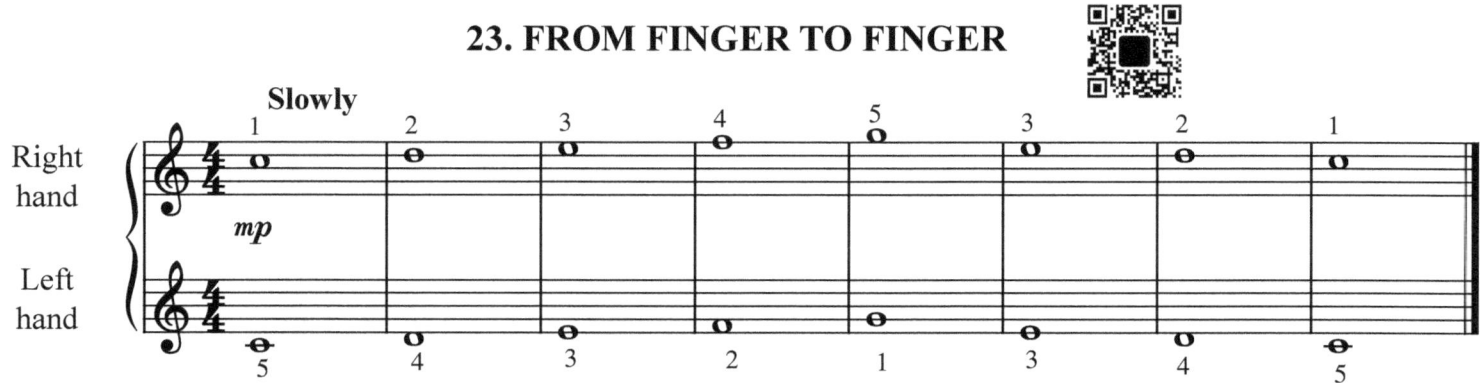

While you count, "One, two, three, four!", one whole note sounds and one measure ends. Don't forget that you are counting for both hands at once. Make sure that the fingers of both hands press the keys at the same time as you count. Both hands play the same melody. The right hand plays one octave higher.

## 24. THROUGH THE FINGER

**Slowly**

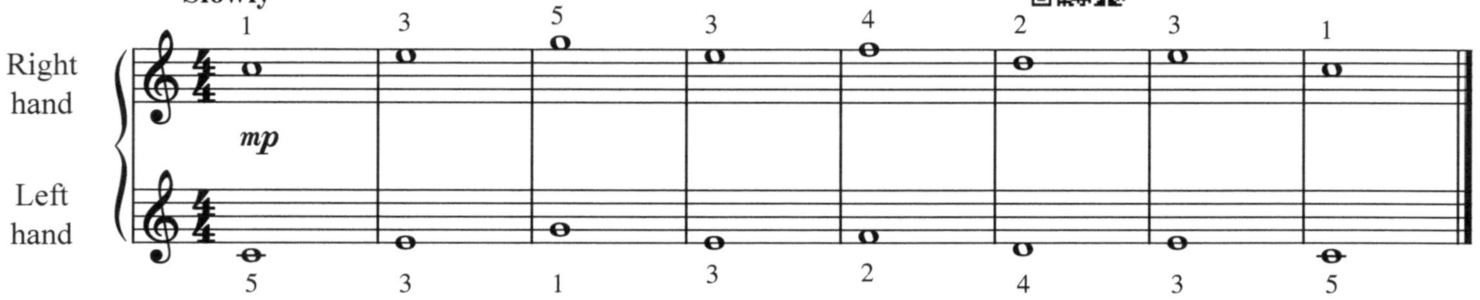

## 25. IN THE FOREST

**On the theme of a German song**

Arranged by J. Mercer

**Slowly**

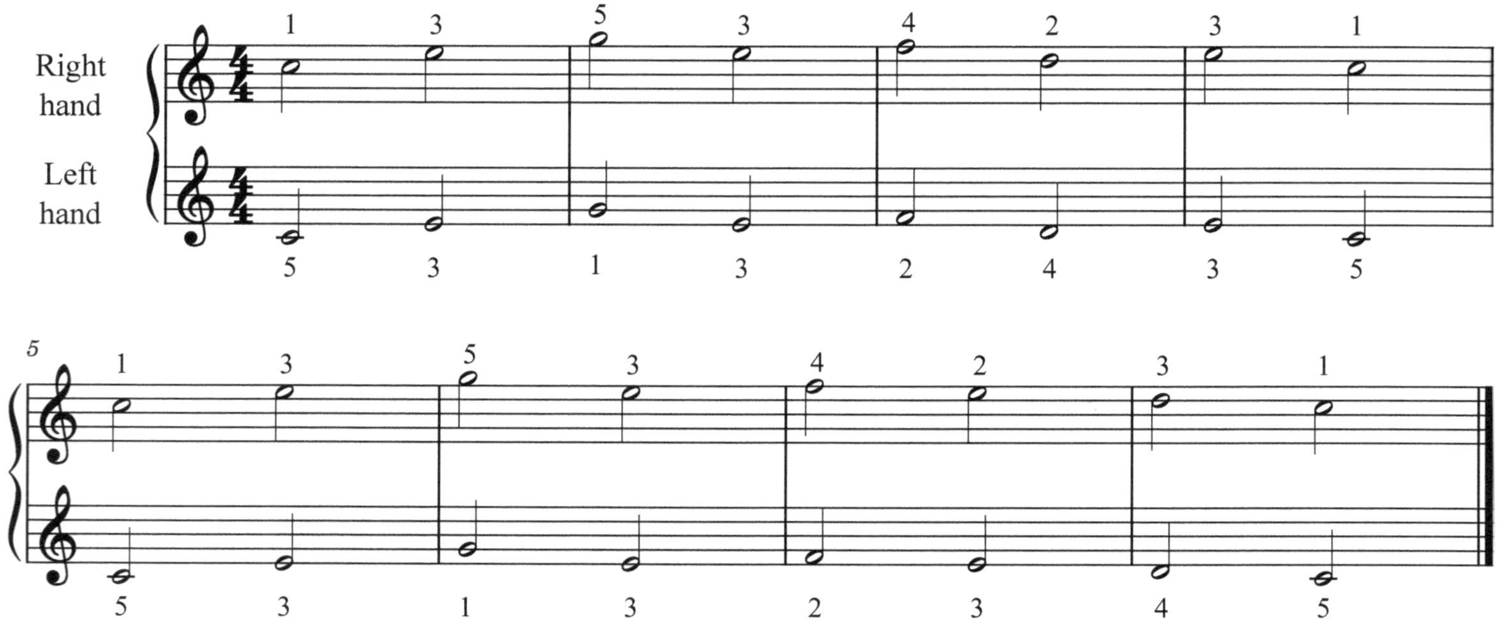

If you can't play a piece with both hands at once, learn the notes of the upper staff first and play only with your right hand. Then learn the notes of the lower staff and play only with your left hand, and only then play with both hands at once. *When learning new pieces you can always do this.*

## 26. EVENING BELL
### On the theme of the song of the same name

Arranged by J. Mercer

This piece shows how beautifully bells sound. Try to hear this ringing.

The last measures do not indicate the finger numbers. Choose the fingers you need yourself. In the 7th and 8th measures, the notes "jump" from the 1st to the 5th finger of the right hand and from the 5th finger to the 1st of the left hand. Therefore, make sure that the fingers move correctly. The hand should not rotate or "fall" after the 1st or 5th fingers.

## 27. BEAR

Arranged by J. Mercer

Very often the sign "**C**" is used to denote the size "four quarters".

43

Before playing pieces with quarter notes, learn these exercises. Play them at a speed that is comfortable for you.

## 28. 12 Little Exercises
### For the right hand

### For the left hand

At the end of each exercise there is a special sign ⫶‖ . This sign is called REPRISE. If it is at the very end of the piece, then it must be repeated from beginning to end. If it is in the middle, then only part of the piece must be repeated - from one sign ‖⫶ to the second sign ⫶‖ .

Play each exercise several times to develop the fingers of the right and left hands.

Count out loud. Emphasise the FIRST quarter of each measure STRONGER. For this purpose there are accent marks (stresses) in the notes.

Constantly monitor the correct position of the hand and fingers. Pay special attention to the 1st and 5th fingers.

## 29. "BLIND" RAIN
### On the theme of a German folk song

Arranged by J. Mercer

Count quarter notes and play EVENLY. Remember the main rule: never adjust the count to the movement of your fingers, but always adjust the movements of your fingers to your count.

When you play, do not be afraid of the notes. Do not "stick" your eyes to them. Notes are just a musical alphabet, musical letters. They are almost the same as letters in ordinary books. Therefore, pay special attention to your hands. They "make" the music. Let your hands be light and relaxed, and let your fingers move easily and correctly.

Do not strain yourself either - no one has ever made good music immediately and without effort.

## 30. MOON "BUNNIES"
### On the theme of a German folk song

Arranged by J. Mercer

## 31. THE BEE
### German folk song

Arranged by J. Mercer

## 32. SLEEP, DELICATE FLOWERS
### German folk song

Arranged by J. Mercer

# PIECES IN THE TREBLE CLEF WITH "DIFFERENT" NOTES FOR EACH HAND

## 33. ON THE SWING
### German folk song

Arranged by J. Mercer

The upper staff has half and whole notes, and the lower staff has only whole notes. This means that both your hands should play their own notes. This is how the piano is most often played - the right hand plays the main or principal melody, and the left hand plays the ACCOMPANIMENT.

It turns out that the left hand accompanies the right hand and "marches" with it in the same company. And since both hands "march" across the keys in the same company, they should move at the same tempo and with the same overall count.

## 34. IN THE COURTYARD
### On the theme of a German folk song

Arranged by J. Mercer

The six ligature signs connect the notes in all the measures on the upper staff, and therefore the right hand must play *legato* six times in a row. *Note*: the ligature does not connect the notes at random. The ligature connects precisely those notes that, like lines in a poem, make up a musical PHRASE. And from these phrases the overall MELODY is formed.

## 35. ROUND DANCE
### German folk song

Arranged by J. Mercer

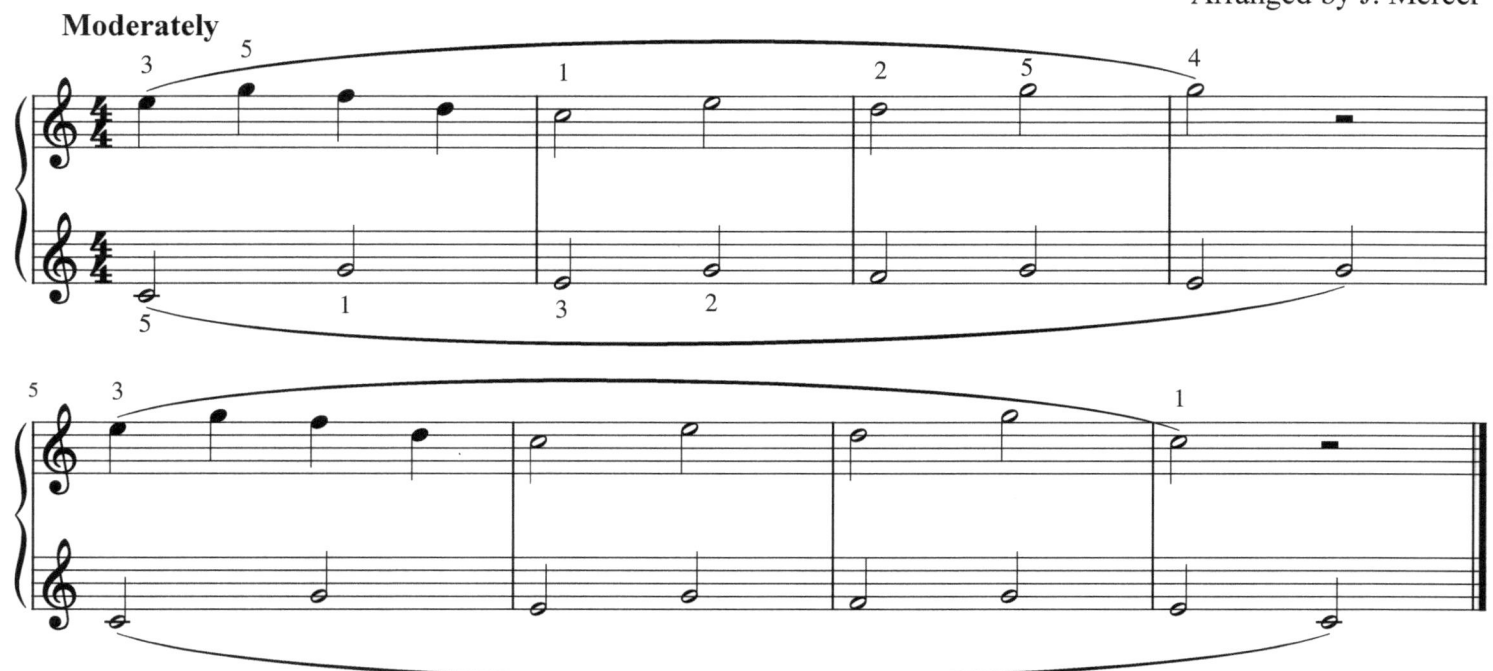

The melody of the piece consists of two phrases united by two slurs. Each phrase from beginning to end should be played legato. In the 3rd and 4th measures, two G notes of the second octave stand next to each other under one common slur. These two notes should be played legato. But it is not very convenient to "step over" from the 5th finger to the same 5th finger again! Therefore, it is better to play the second G note in the 4th measure with another finger. The closest is the 4th finger. To press the G key a second time, smoothly "step over" from the 5th to the 4th finger, as indicated 1 in the notes and in this figure.

## 36. ROLLERBLADES
### German folk song

Arranged by J. Mercer

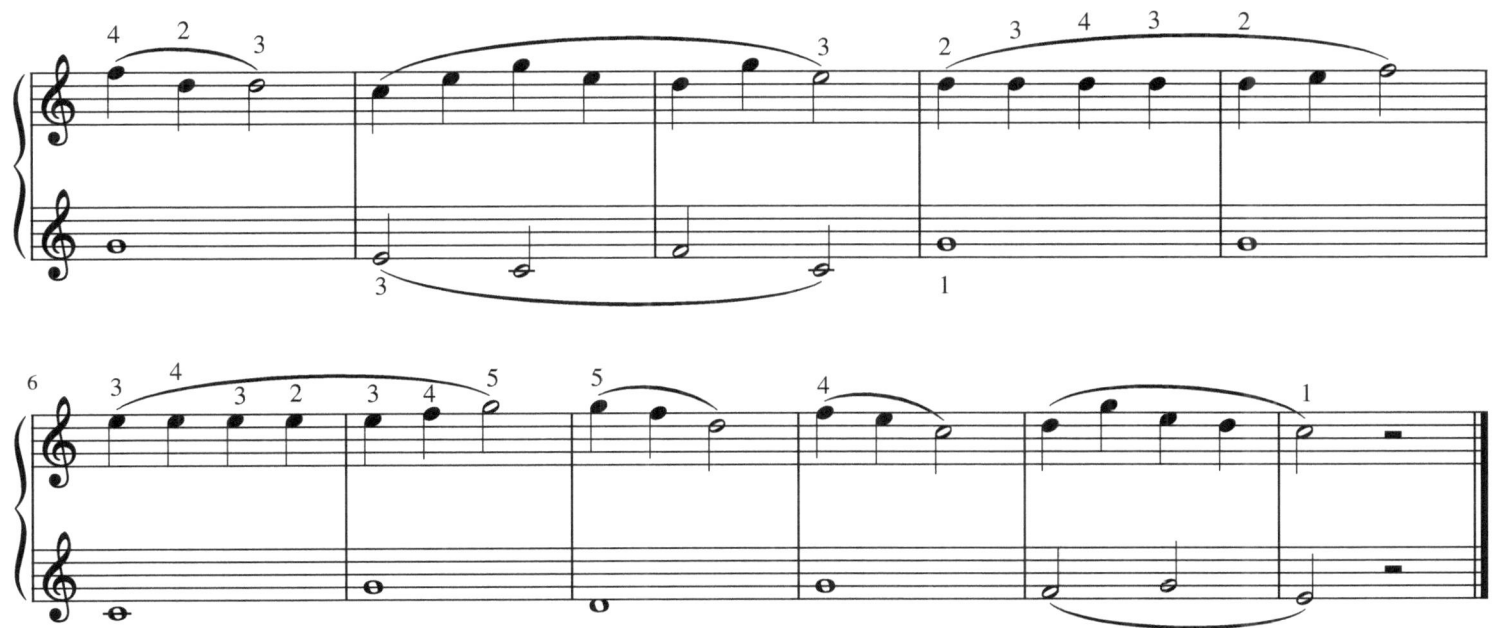

In the 5th, 6th, 9th and 11th measures, the ligature unites identical notes standing next to each other. In order for such notes to sound smoothly and coherently, it can be inconvenient to press them with the same finger. In order not to "pound" the key several times with the same finger, it is better to press identical notes in turn with the closest fingers, and "step over" from one to another, as indicated in the notes. When playing in the usual "non legato" way, they often do the same - identical, adjacent notes are pressed with different fingers.

## 37. IN THE FOREST

Arranged by J. Mercer

**Slowly**

49

In the 3rd and 7th measures of the lower staff you see a new note. This note is from the LEFT side of the keyboard. It is located immediately to the left of the middle C key, as shown in this picture. This is the note B, and it is written under the 1st additional line of the staff. You will play this note B with the 5th finger of your left hand.

In the 8th, last measure on the upper staff there are two identical notes C. It is better to play them with different fingers.

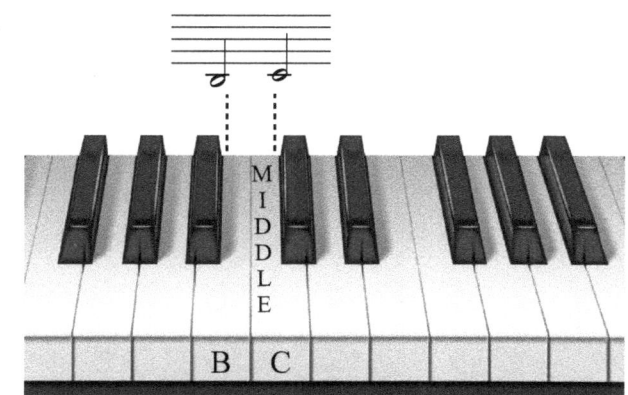

### 38. CUCKOO
**German folk song**

Arranged by J. Mercer

In the 9th and 11th measures the same notes D and the same notes E are next to each other. It is better to press these keys with different fingers.

### 39. DISCO

Arranged by J. Mercer

On the lower staff in each measure next to the HALF note there is a DOT, as shown in this picture.

A dot placed to the right of a half note lengthens the duration of this note by exactly HALF or exactly ONE quarter. You can consider that one quarter note was added to the half note and a new note was obtained. This new note is called "half with a dot". It has a duration equal to three quarter notes and is counted in three counts: "One, two, three!" If the measure has a size of " $\frac{3}{4}$ ", then the half with a dot is equal to the duration of one measure. This is exactly how all the measures on the lower staff are written in the play.

## 40. WALTZ OF THE DOLLS
### Austrian folk dance

Arranged by J. Mercer

In the 2nd, 4th and 12th measures there are half notes with a dot. Count these notes on three counts and they will sound throughout the entire measure. In the 8th measure on the count "two, three!" for the right hand there is a "silent" note - a half rest.

# LEARN TO PLAY PIECES WITH VERY SHORT NOTES

A very important note in music is a quarter note. Because one quarter note is one beat in measures of $\frac{2}{4}$, $\frac{3}{4}$ and $\frac{4}{4}$, and one quarter note is equal to one "one!" beat.

If a quarter note sounds for two beats, it is a half note. If you "force" a quarter note to sound for three beats, you get a half note with a dot. If a quarter note sounds for all four beats, you get a full note. And what happens if you divide a quarter note in half into two short notes? Then the music becomes richer, because it will have new very short sounds. To get very short notes, the duration of one quarter note is divided into two equal parts, and you get two short notes, as shown in the picture. The new notes are called EIGHTH notes. They look the same as quarter notes, but they have an extra tail on top. These notes are called eighth notes because in one whole note there are exactly EIGHT such notes "hidden". You can count and see for yourself.
You should get everything as in this picture.

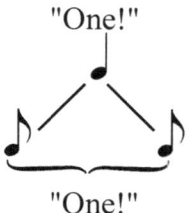

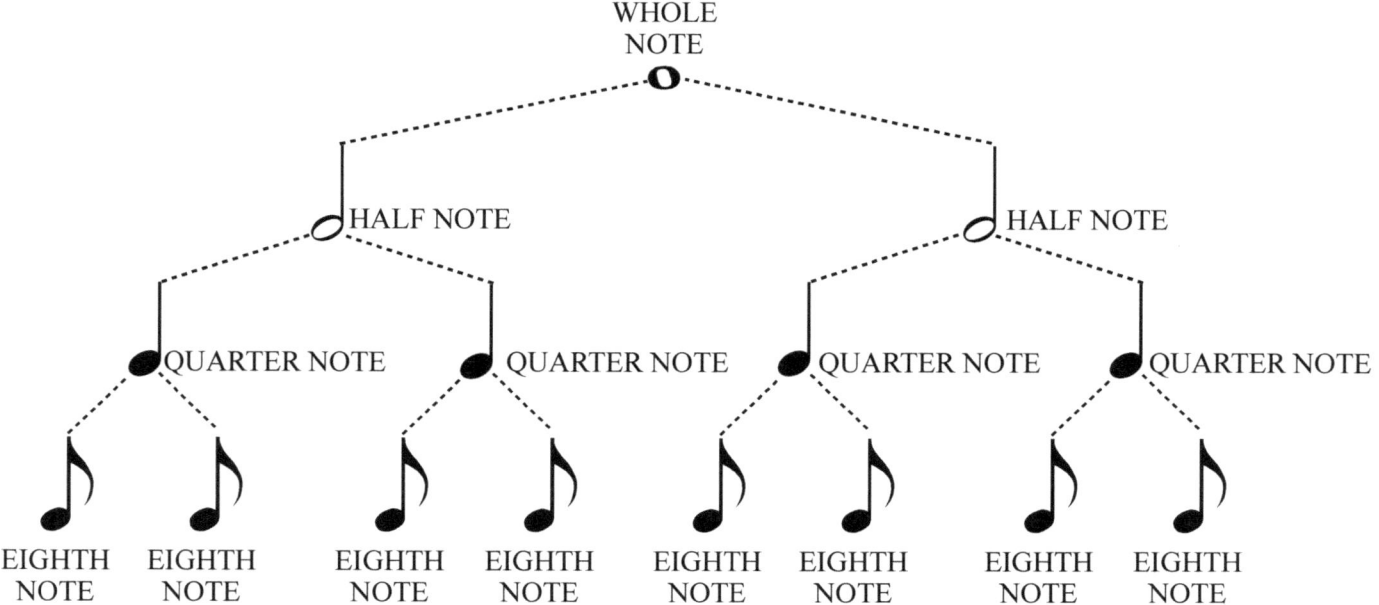

Very often, for convenience, eighth notes are depicted in whole "bundles" of two, three, four, or even more, as shown in this picture. The crossbar that binds the eighth notes is called a "bundle."

One quarter note is one count - "one". Therefore, the eighth note should sound exactly half of your count. What to do? To do this, one count "one" must be divided in half using the word - "And". In one count, you need to have time to say: "ONE - AND!" and press the keys twice, in the second count say: "TWO - AND!" and also press the keys twice, in the third count - "THREE - AND!", in the fourth count - "FOUR - AND!" And so on for each count press the keys twice.

Count eighth notes as shown in this picture.

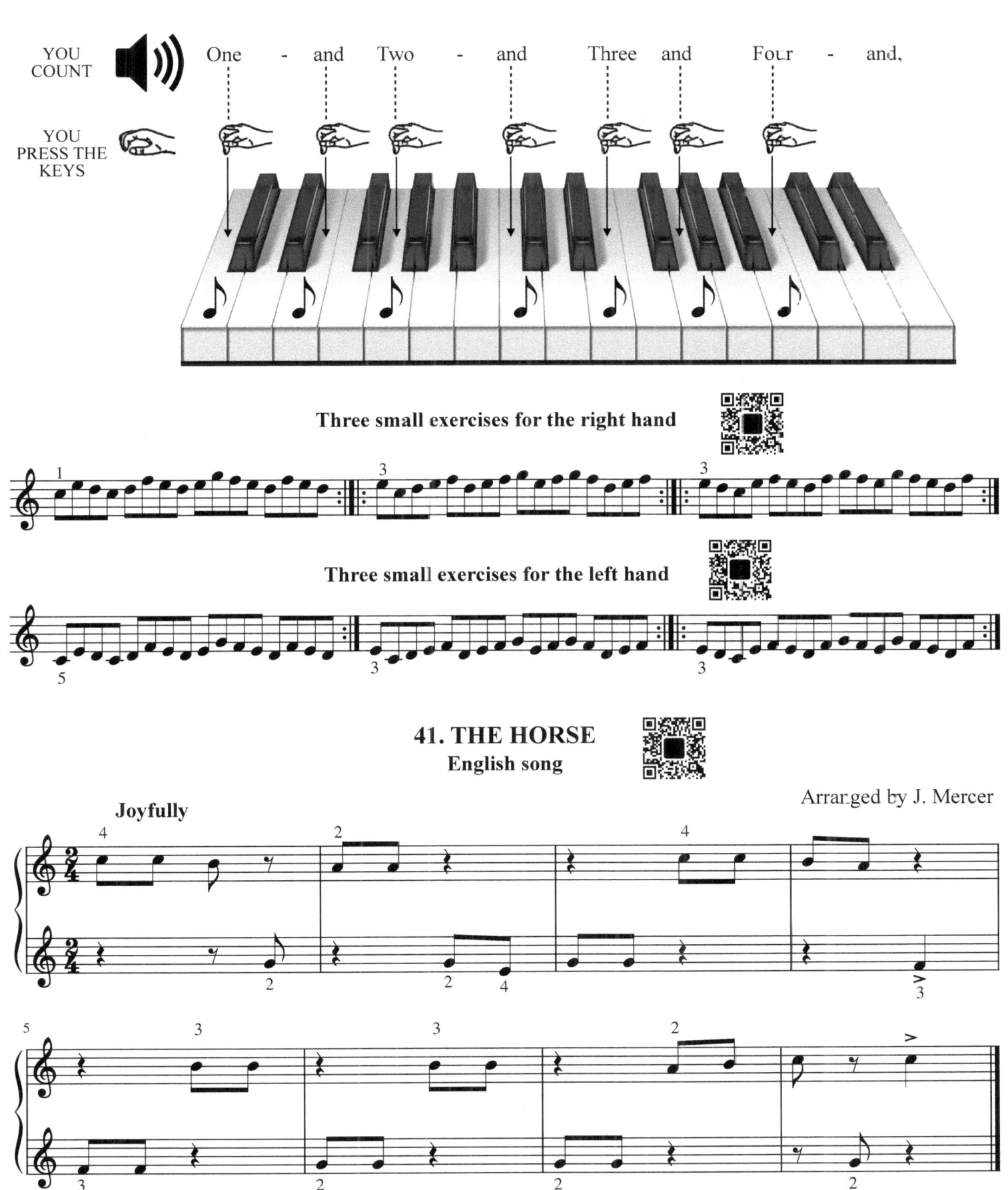

**Three small exercises for the right hand**

**Three small exercises for the left hand**

## 41. THE HORSE
### English song

Arranged by J. Mercer

**Joyfully**

In the 1st and 8th measures of the piece "The Horse" you see new signs: ⅞. These are eighth rests. Like other rests: whole, half and quarter, they interrupt the sound of the melody. The duration of the eighth rest is equal to the duration of the eighth note, and therefore these rests are also counted by dividing one count in half: "One-And", "Two-And", etc.

*Note:* there is no break in the sound in this piece, because while one hand is not playing ("silent"), the other plays.

## 42. BY THE FOREST STREAM

Arranged by J. Mercer

Count eighth notes the same way you just did. For every quarter note in your left hand, there are two eighth notes in your right hand.

## 43. BY THE FOREST BROOK

Learn and play the piece "By the Forest Brook" using new notes. The melody is now played by the left hand, and the right hand plays the accompaniment.

**Slowly**

54

## 11. KITTEN ON THE KEYS

Arranged by J. Mercer

In the first part of the piece, the right hand plays EIGHTH notes, and the left hand plays HALF notes. In the second part, it's the other way around - the left hand plays EIGHTH notes, and the right hand plays HALF notes. But in both the first and second parts, there are four eighth notes per half note, and they should sound as long as one half note. The piece should be played non legato because the kitten runs across the keys very unsmoothly.

## 45. GOOD MORNING EVERYONE!

Arranged by J. Mercer

In measures 6 and 7 of the piece there is a new ⌐ sign for you. The note above or below which this sign is located must be played especially clearly. The key must be pressed vigorously and the full duration of the note must be maintained.

## 46. ON A BICYCLE

Arranged by J. Mercer

**Moderately**

The melody in this piece should be played *legato* because the bicycle almost always moves smoothly.

In the 2nd measure you change the position of your right hand over the keys and move your hand one key to the right. Then the 1st finger will be over the D key of the second octave, as indicated in the notes. In the second half of the 4th measure, there is a half rest on the upper staff. During the time that your right hand is "silent", you should play four eighth notes with your left hand.

In the 7th measure you play the B note on the upper staff with the 1st finger.

# PIECES IN THE TREBLE AND BASS CLEF FOR TWO HANDS

This picture shows the left side of the keyboard. It is arranged in the same way as the right side.

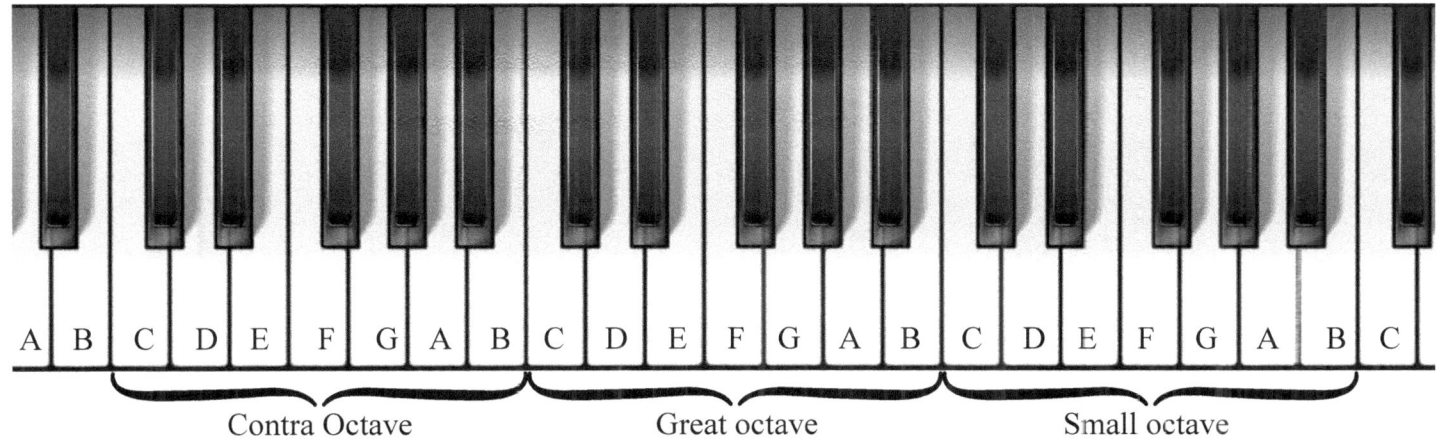

To the left of the C middle key there are three octaves, which are called: SMALL, GREAT, and CONTRA OCTAVE. The three leftmost "extra" keys - two white and one black - are part of an incomplete SUBCONTR-OCTAVE.

To play on the left side of the keyboard you need to remember how the keys of the SMALL and GREAT octaves are located on the keyboard and the notes of these octaves on the lower staff.

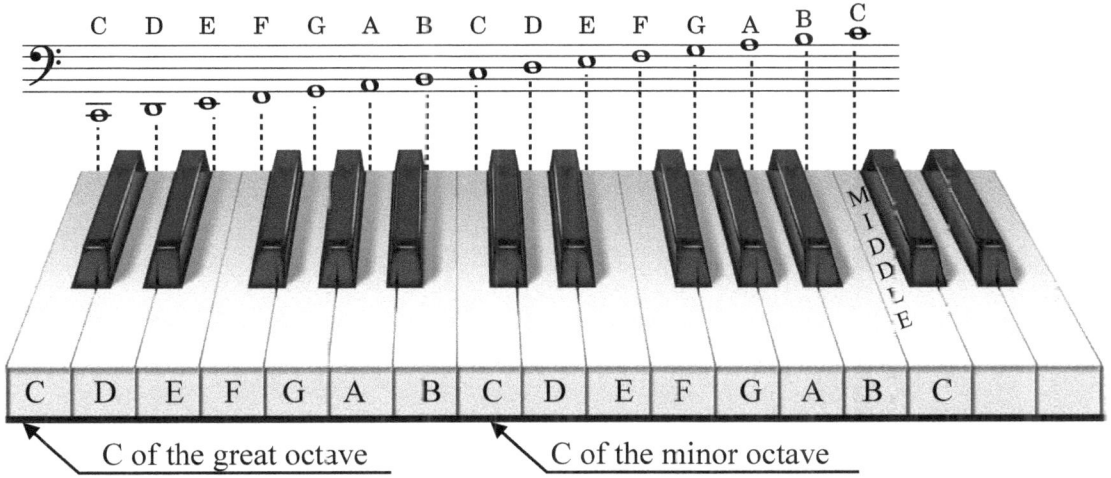

The left part of the keyboard is usually played with the left hand, and that is why the lower staff is shown in the picture. At the very beginning of this staff there is also a "key" "hanging". This "key" is called the the Bass Clef, and it "locks" the FOURTH line so that it is immediately clear that this line is occupied by the note F of the SMALL octave as shown in this picture. Learn to draw the Bass clef as shown in this picture. Trace the Bass clef that is already drawn.

Look at the drawing of the staff and remember how the notes of the small and large octaves are located on the LOWER staff and the keys on the LEFT part of the keyboard.

Move your eyes from left to right - first along the top line, then along the bottom. Mentally pronounce the names of all the notes in a row - on the lines and in the spaces between the lines. Repeat this "walk" 5 times, each time increasing the speed of movement.

With the 2nd or 3rd finger of your left hand press the keys in order and loudly call out each note "by name". "Walk" with your eyes along the notes, and with your finger along the keys 5 times. Each time try to do it faster.

Practice this before each lesson until you begin, almost without thinking, to call all the notes of the small octave and half the notes of the large octave "by name" and press the necessary keys.

Look at the large picture on the next page, which contains the entire scale of your piano.

High notes, starting from middle C and above, are written on the UPPER staff. Low notes, starting from middle C and below, are written on the LOWER staff. The entire scale consists of SEVEN octaves and four "extra" keys - the far right key and the three far left keys. You don't need to know the location of all these notes and keys yet. You won't need many of these sounds for a long time.

To play well with your right hand, the keys of the First, Second and half of the Third octave will be enough for you. And to play well with your left hand, the Small and half of the Large octave will be enough for you to begin with. Therefore, among all the keys of the piano, these are your best friends. These sounds and keys are for a pianist what the heart is for a person. Therefore, you should be able to see the location of the keys and notes in this "heart" even with your eyes closed. To make it easier for you to understand how the "heart" of your piano scale is arranged, this "heart" is shown on a separate page.

This picture shows how two staves are connected together - the upper one with the Treble clef and the lower one with the Treble clef. To prevent these two staves from "losing" each other, they were fastened, like with a paper clip, with a common middle line, and the note C middle was placed on this common line. Therefore, it turned out that the middle line, on which C middle "hangs", became a common additional line for TWO staves at once. For the upper staff, this is the lower first additional line, and for the lower staff, the upper first additional line.

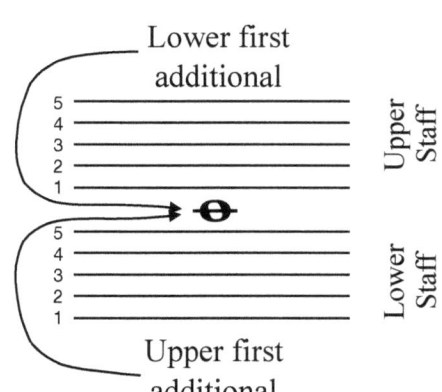

# FULL SCALE OF YOUR PIANO

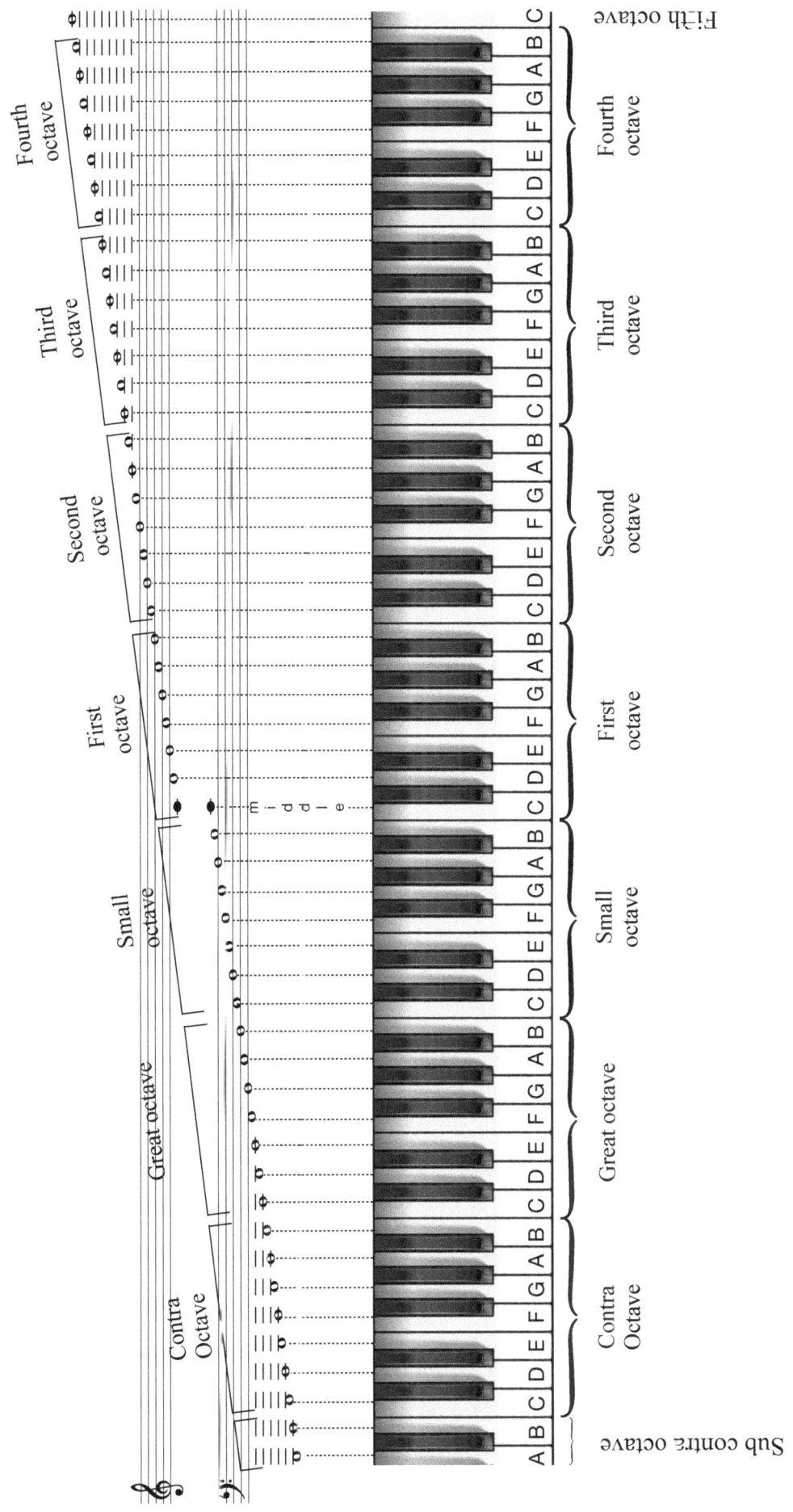

59

# "THE HEART" OF THE SOUND CHORD

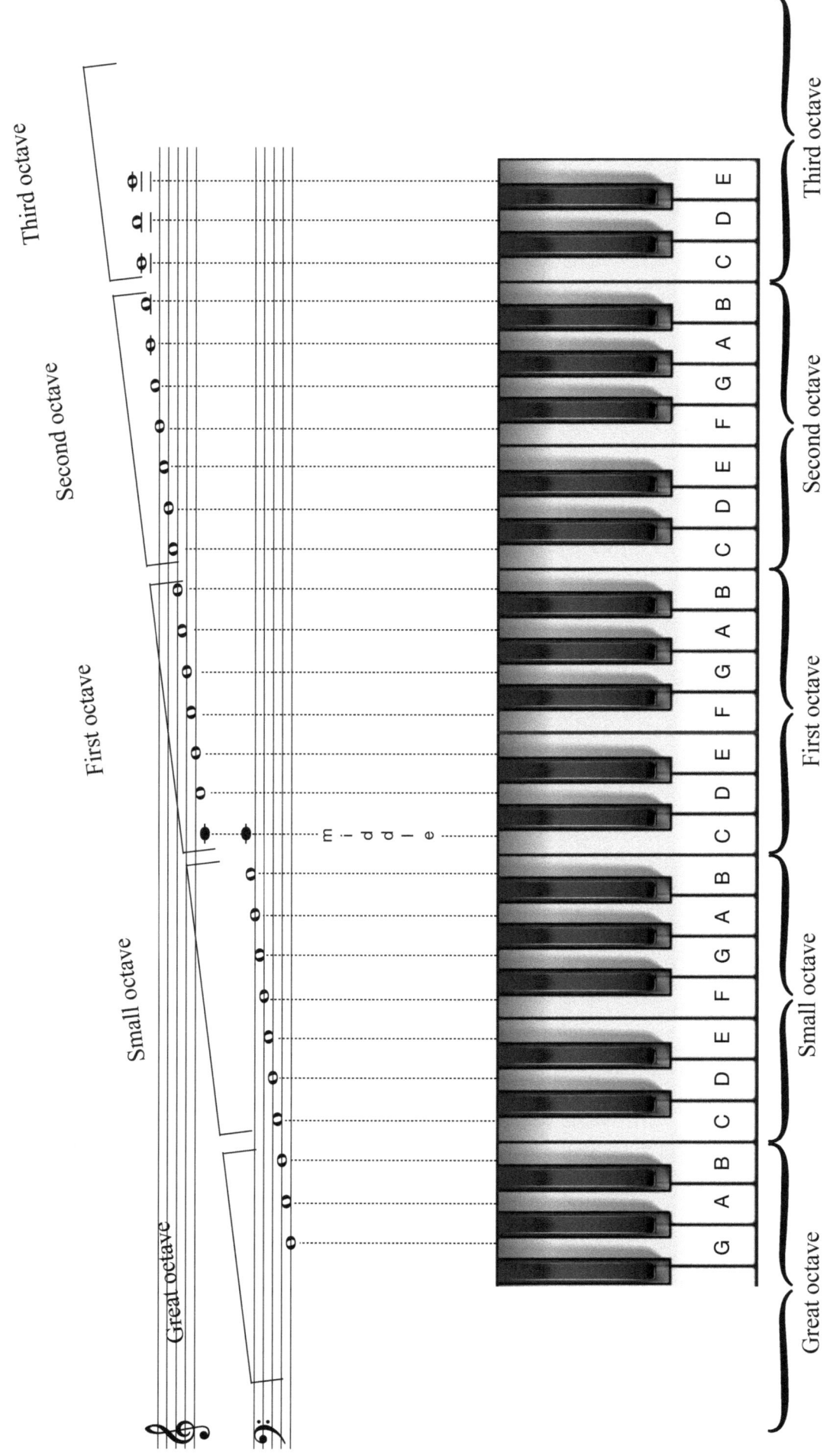

**And this drawing helps you quickly remember how the notes are located on the upper and lower staves.**

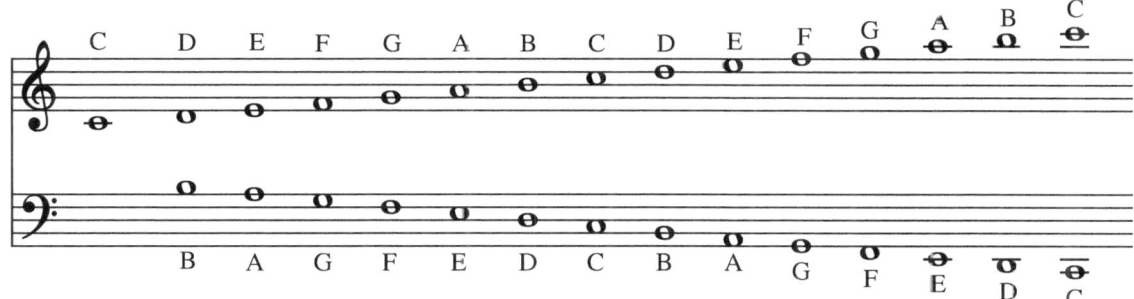

Please note: the notes C of different octaves written on the upper and lower staves are reflected as if in a mirror.

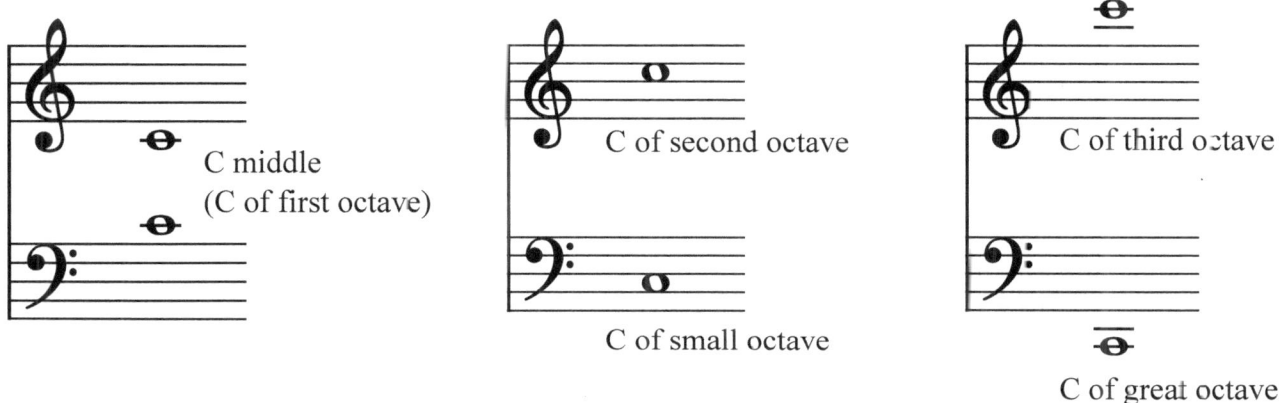

Before playing pieces in the Treble clef and in the Bass clef with both hands position your chair correctly opposite the MIDDLE of the keyboard.

## 47. BREEZE FROM THE SEA
### American melody "Breeze"

Arranged by J. Mercer

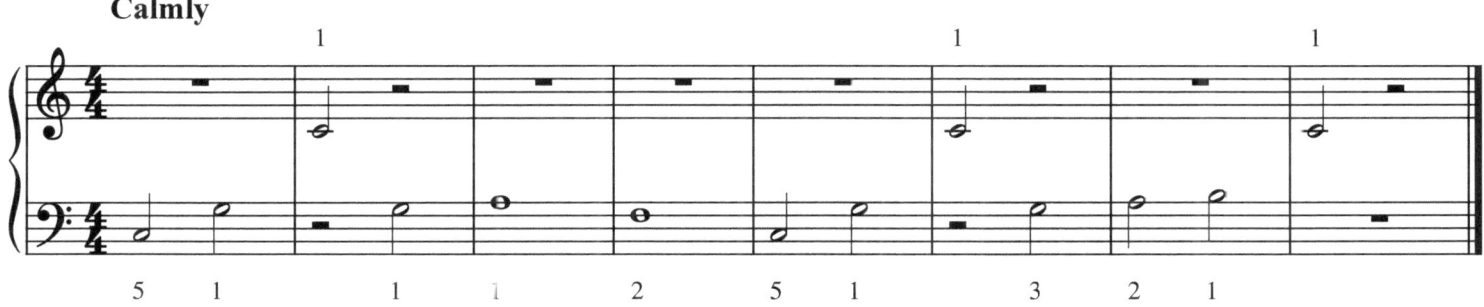

## 48. EVENING

Arranged by J. Mercer

## 49. LEFT HAND DOWN AND UP

Arranged by J. Mercer

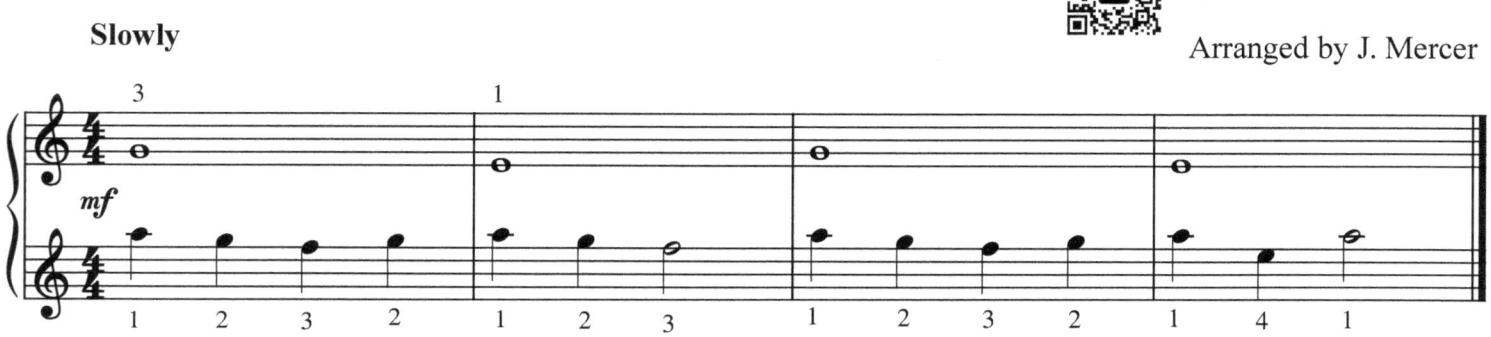

## 50. LEFT HAND UP AND DOWN

Arranged by J. Mercer

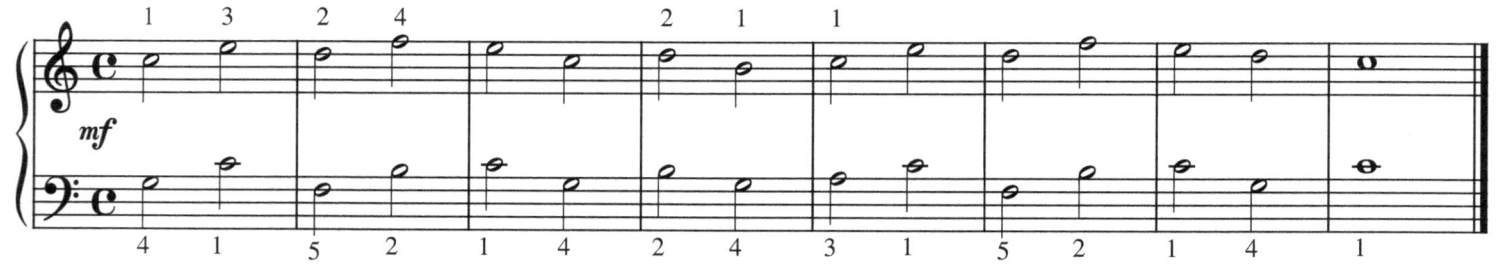

Distribute your fingers on the keys of the Small and First Octaves as shown in this picture. Touch the keys with your fingertips.

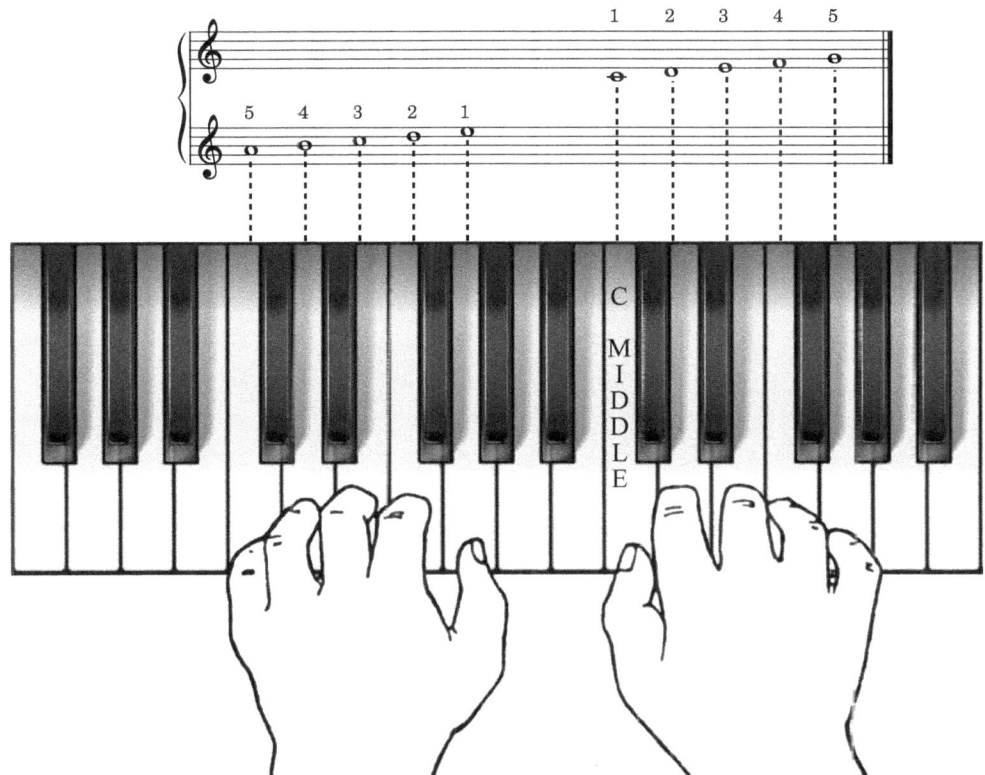

This arrangement of the fingers on the keys is called - C MAJOR POSITION. "C" is the name of the note C. The 1st finger of your right hand and the 5th finger of your left hand are ready to play the note C, which will appear in the most important places of the piece. The word "major" comes from the Latin words 'large' and "hard". And this means that in this position your fingers should play energetic, cheerful music.

You are familiar with the C major position. You have already played in this position. It's just that now your hands have moved to the left exactly one octave. But before, all ten of your fingers played in the Treble Clef. And now five fingers of your left hand will play in the Bass clef. On the lower staff, "locked" to the Bass clef, all the notes have changed their names. You know how this happened and you will quickly get used to it. Look at the picture and remember how the keys are connected to the notes, and your fingers to the keys. From this point on, you will play increasingly complex and interesting pieces. Always remember how to do it with the help of three letters of the alphabet.

A. Never start PLAYING until you are sure that you already know EXACTLY how you will begin, continue and end the piece. To do this, you must know how many measures there are in the piece, what notes are in them, how these notes should be counted, with which fingers and in what way you should play (legato or non legato).

B. Learn the notes of a complex piece first for the right hand, then for the left, and only after that play the piece with both hands. While you are learning the piece, count out loud. When you have learned it, count silently. Count EVENLY and never ADJUST the count to your playing, but adjust the playing to an even count. Remember that you are counting for both hands at the same time - RIGHT and LEFT - and for two staves - UPPER and LOWER. If you cannot play at a faster tempo, do not get upset and play the piece as fast as you can. The main thing is to count EVENLY and play CORRECTLY.

C. Even when you are learning a piece, constantly make sure that your fingers move along the keys in the CORRECT position. The position of the 1st finger is very important for all the others. Therefore, the 1st finger should always be slightly rounded, as if it always wants to "hide" under the 2nd finger. Watch your 1st fingers. The 3rd finger is always moved closer to the black keys than all the other fingers.

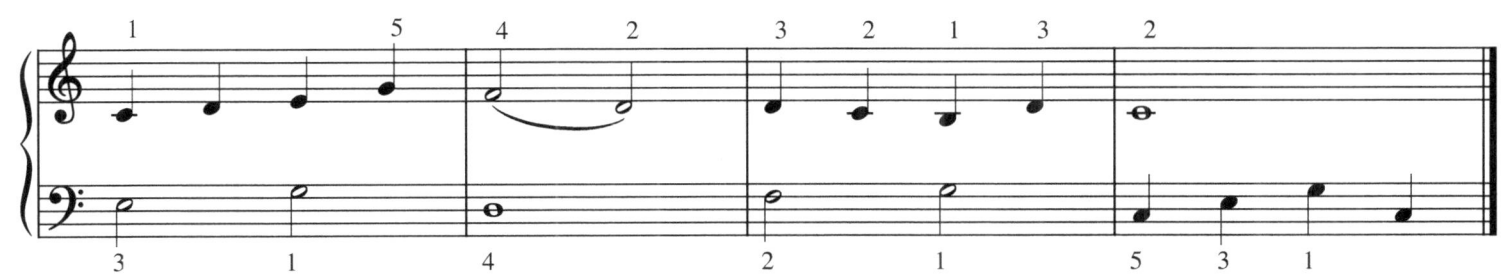

## 54. ELEPHANT

Arranged by J. Mercer

**Slowly**

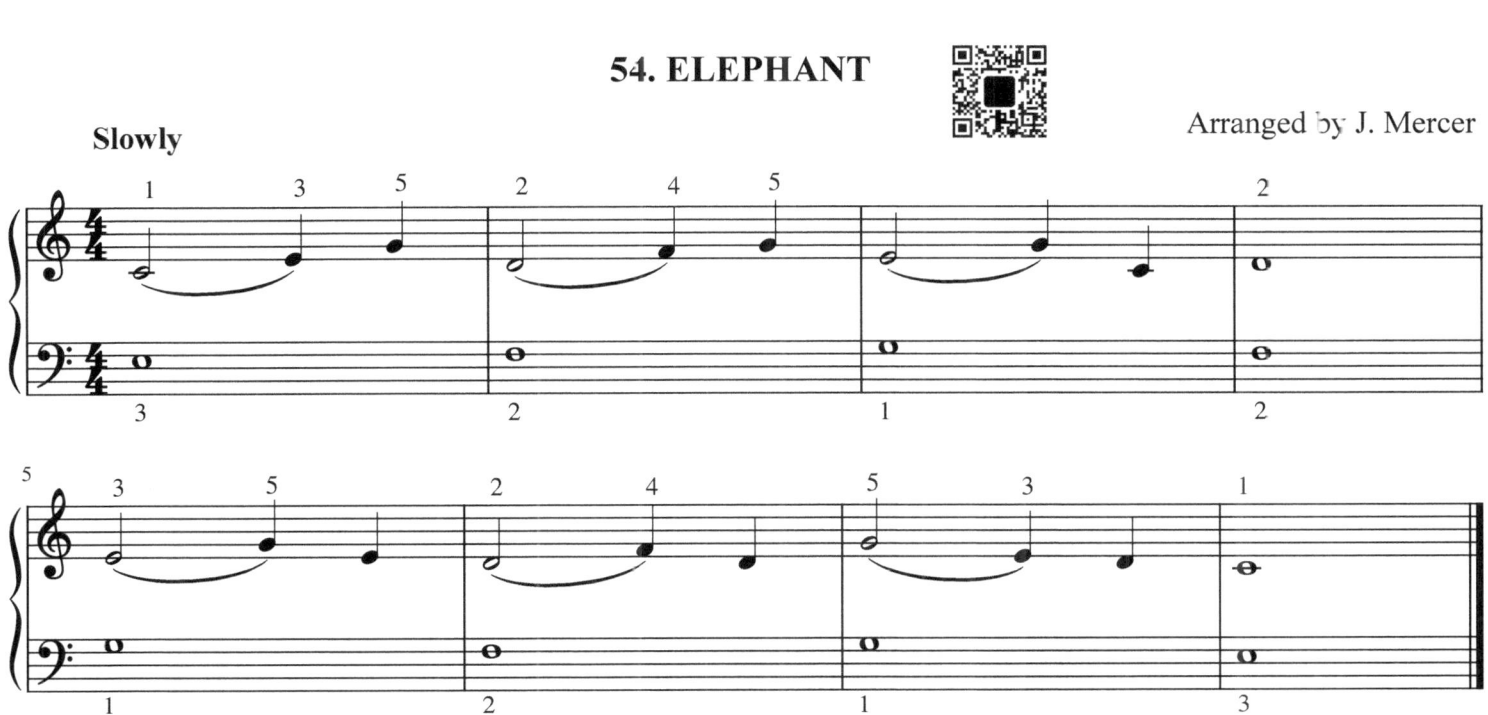

## 55. ON THE RIVER
**Canadian song "Beaver"**

Arranged by J. Mercer

**Calmly**

## 56. SUNSET

Arranged by J. Mercer

**Calmly**

## 57. "VALENTINE"

Arranged by J. Mercer

**In waltz tempo**

## 58. BALLOON

Arranged by J. Mercer

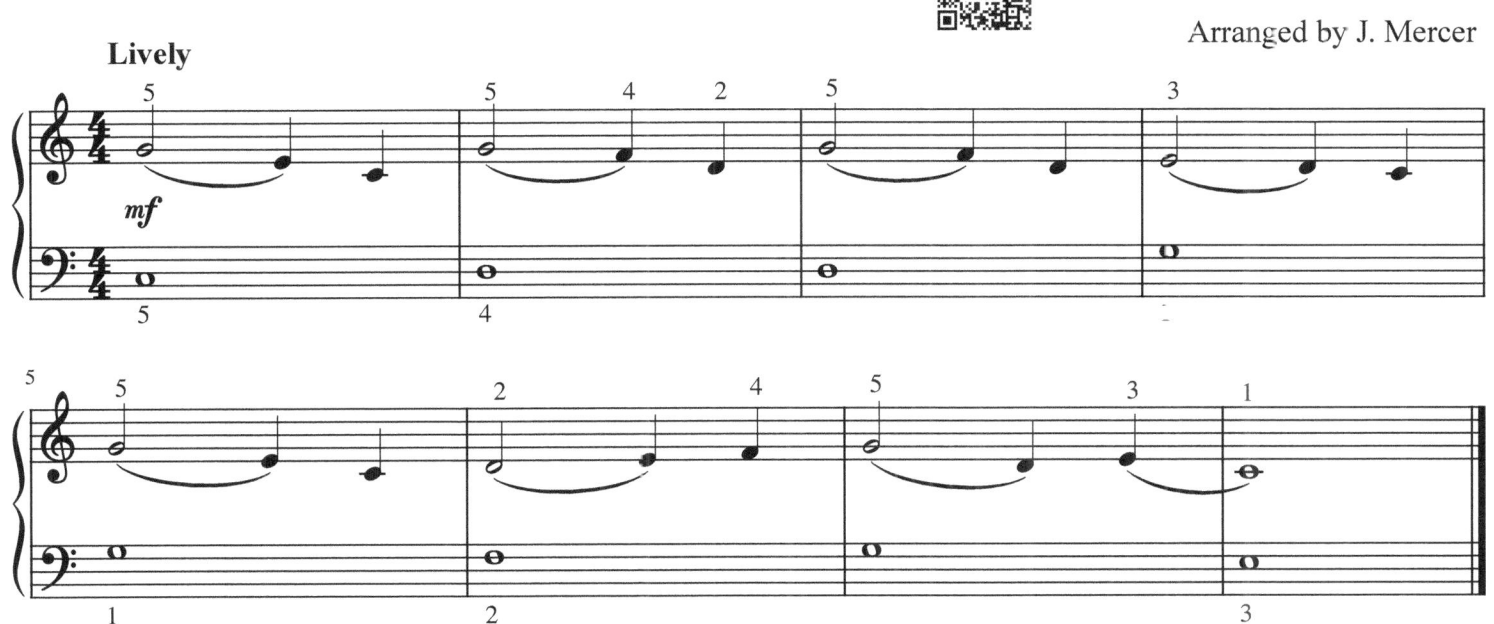

# LEARN TO MOVE YOUR HAND IN THE "C MAJOR" POSITION

Very often in the position of C major, the note C middle (C of the First Octave) should be played not with the right, but with the left hand. To do this, the left hand is moved to the right close to the right hand, so that the 1st finger of the left hand is also above the key C middle, as shown in the picture.

Both fingers will not press the key C middle at the same time, but in turn. The key B of the Small Octave is pressed by the 2nd finger of the left hand. The keys A, G and F are pressed by the 3rd, 4th and 5th fingers.

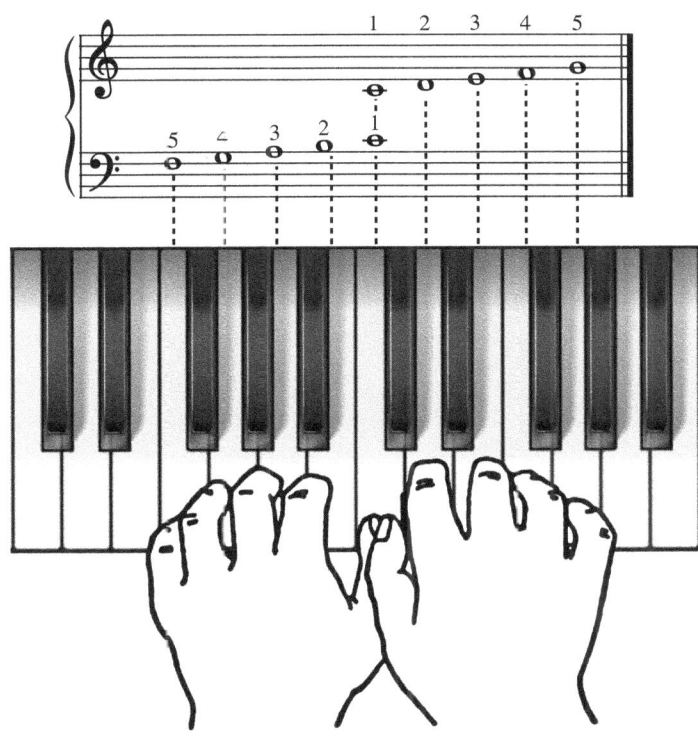

## 59. BUTTERFLY

Arranged by J. Mercer

In this piece, the slurs span the notes on the upper staff, then descend to the lower staff. This means that the musical phrase begins on the upper staff, then continues on the lower staff. Legato should be played as the slur indicates.

In measures 6 and 7 on the lower staff, two identical notes, G of the minor octave, are next to each other, and therefore are best played with different fingers.

## 60. ALARM CLOCK
### Canadian song

Arranged by J. Mercer

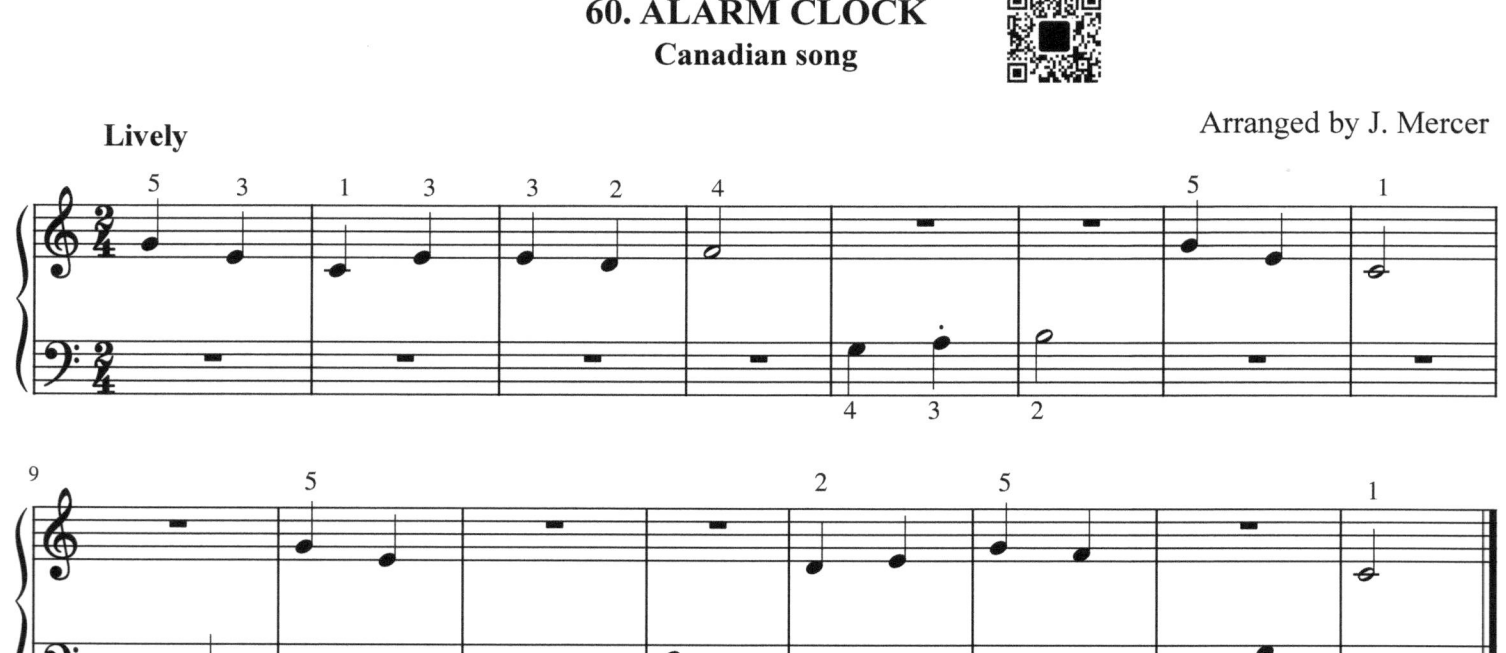

In the 5th and 6th measures the left hand moves to the right. From the 9th measure it returns to the left.

# 61. EVENING

Arranged by J. Mercer

**Slowly**

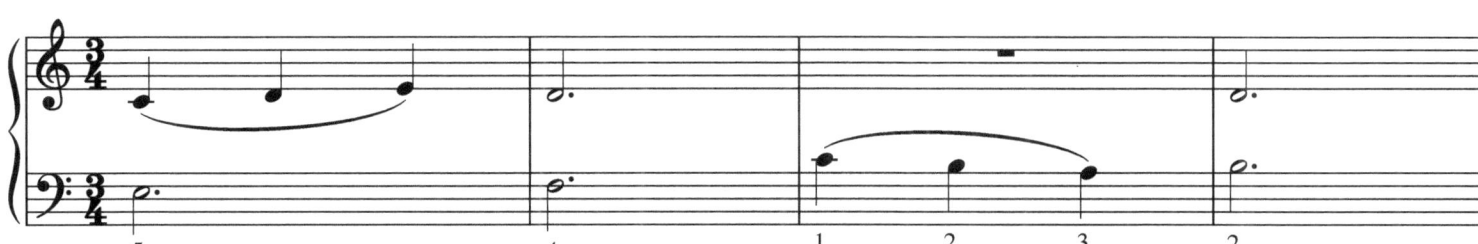

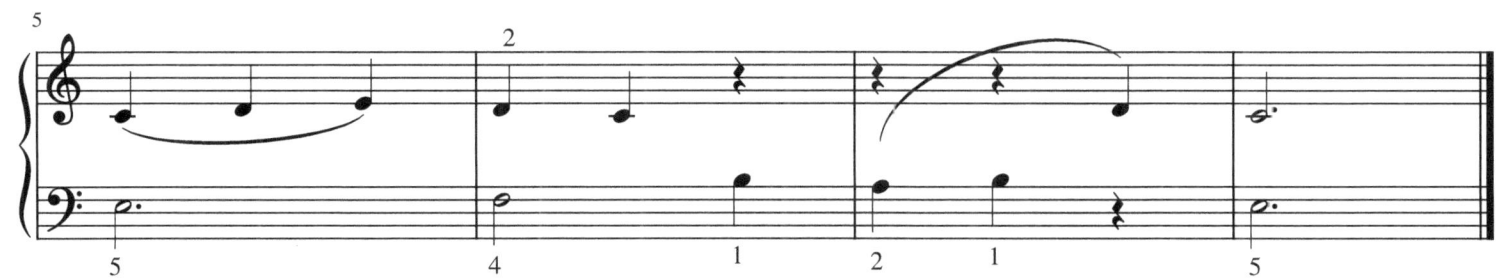

# 62. SUNNY DAY
### French song

Arranged by J. Mercer

**Moderately**

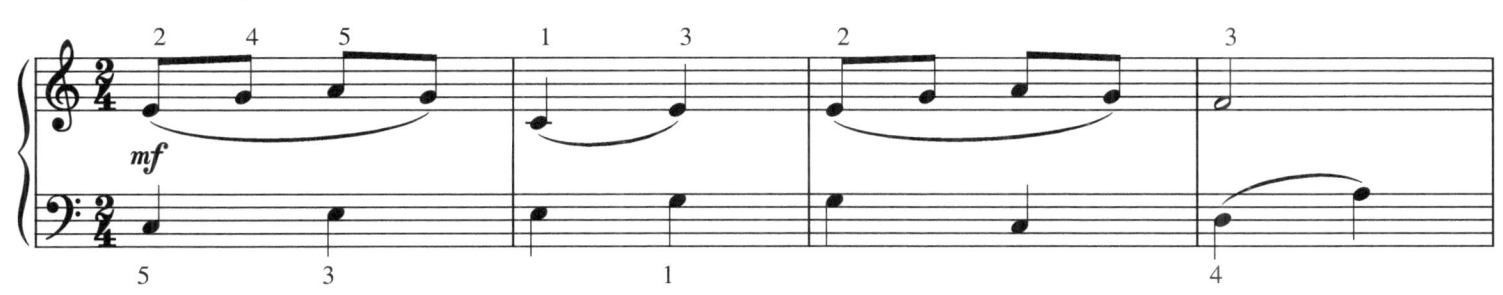

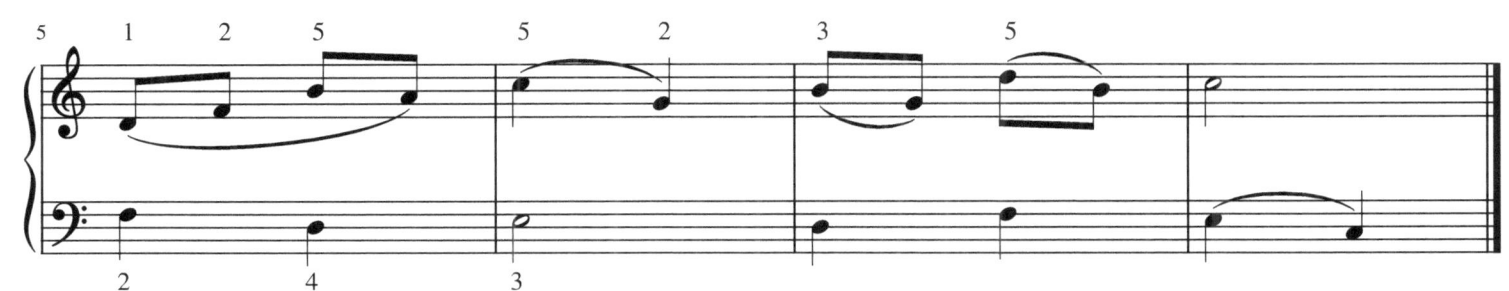

## 63. AT THE SEA
### American song "Hannah"

Calmly

Arranged by J. Mercer

The waves on the sea roll smoothly, and therefore the piece is played legato. In the 10th and 11th measures there are signs of a whole rest, and therefore the right hand does not play in these measures. Note: the sign of a whole rest is put when the rest should last a whole measure. This sign is put equally for measures with a duration of "four quarters" and "three quarters". For measures in "two quarters" the sign of a half rest is put, but the sign of a whole rest is also allowed.

## 64. SILENT NIGHT
### French song

Arranged by J. Mercer

Slowly

In the 5th measure, the slur sign combines three notes on two staves at once, as shown in this picture. This means that you need to play legato with both hands - start with the right hand and finish with the left. Then it turns out that the melody in the 5th measure smoothly passes from the right hand to the left. The slur almost always combines individual notes of the melody into musical phrases. Therefore, the slur sign not only says: "Play legato, without raising your hand for each new note". This sign also shows where the musical phrase begins and ends.

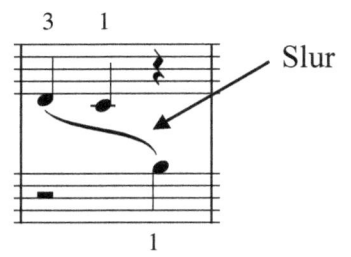

Slur

***Remember the main thing:*** the slur sign helps you understand the language of music. Because a phrase for a melody is the same as a sentence for human speech.

Playing legato in the 5th measure, you must smoothly "step over" from the 1st finger of the right hand to the 1st finger of the left hand. From the 5th measure, the left hand moves to the right, and in the last measure it returns to its previous position.

# LEARN TO PLAY DOUBLE NOTES

To make the piano sound like a whole orchestra, you need to be able to play several legs at once with one hand. You need to learn to do this with your right hand, your left hand, and both hands together.

The picture shows the notes for the right hand.

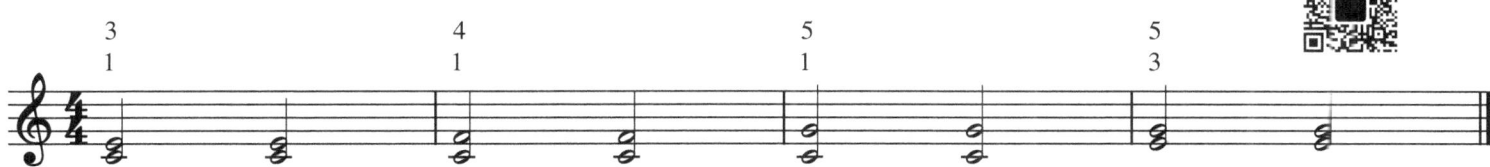

Two half notes stand one above the other. The note above is E of the first octave, below is C middle. Both notes are connected by a common stick. A common stick means that these two notes must be played only together. To do this, you need to press two keys at the same time with two fingers. The numbers next to the notes are the numbers of the fingers with which you need to play these notes. The upper number refers to the upper note, the lower number to the lower note.

With the 1st and 3rd fingers of your right hand, press the C middle and E keys simultaneously. Round the 1st finger slightly. Round all non-playing fingers a little, too, as shown in this picture. Play the 1st measure with the 1st and 3rd fingers several times in a row. Play as many times as you want until both notes start to sound simultaneously and together, without being late or ahead of each other. These two notes should sound like one.

Go to the second measure and play double notes with the 1st and 4th fingers. Then go to the third measure and play double notes with the 1st and 5th fingers. Keep all your fingers rounded - both the two fingers that play and the other three fingers that "hang" freely above the keys.

Hold your fingers as shown in this picture. Be especially careful that the hand does not lean too much towards the 5th finger, and does not "fall" towards the 1st.

Never play double notes with straight fingers, as shown in these two pictures.

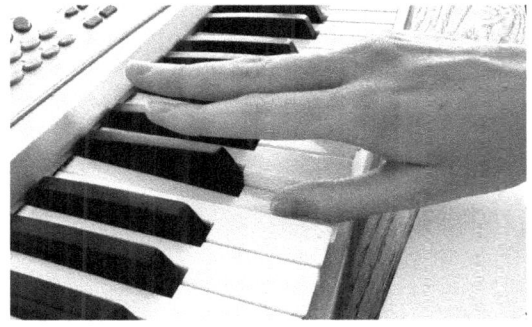

Go to the fourth, most difficult measure, and play double notes with the 3rd and 5th fingers. Play any double notes calmly. Do not tense your fingers, your hand, or your entire arm. Do not tense your body either. Just press the keys so that the two notes start and finish sounding SIMULTANEOUSLY.

When you learn to play each measure separately, play all four measures in a row at a slow tempo and count out loud.

**This picture shows double notes for the left hand.**

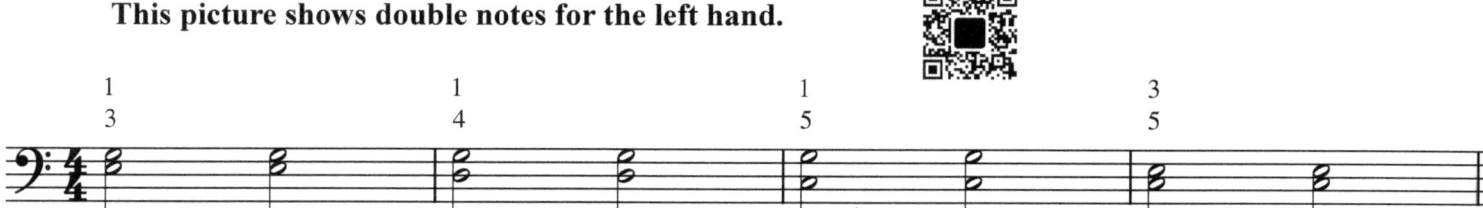

Learn to play each measure separately, then play all four measures in a row at a slow tempo and count out loud. Keep your fingers as shown in the picture.

## 65. DREAM
**French melody**

Arranged by J. Mercer

In the 6th and 7th measures, move your left hand to the right. In this position, play double notes in the 6th measure with the 1st and 2nd fingers of your left hand. In the 5th, 6th and 7th measures, the tie combines notes on two staves at once. Therefore, you will smoothly "step over" from the 2nd finger of your right hand to the 2nd finger of your left hand. In the 8th measure, the left hand returns to its original position.

## 66. RAIN
**Canadian song**

Arranged by J. Mercer

# 67. RINGING BELLS

Arranged by J. Mercer

**Measuredly and solemnly**

# 68. THE KIND LION
### English song

Arranged by J. Mercer

**Moderately**

## 69. HEAVY SUITCASE
### American song "Some Like to Sigh"

Arranged by J. Mercer

In this piece, double notes are to be played with both hands at once. In the first six measures, the left hand plays only the first half of the measure on the count of "one, two", and on the count of "three, four" it maintains half rests. In the 6th measure, there is a double note with a dot on the upper staff. This means that it should sound and be counted on three counts: "one, two, three". The count of "four" in this measure falls on the quarter note F. Note: the dot, which lengthens the half note by another quarter, is placed in the double notes next to each of the two notes.

## 70. UKRAINIAN CHANTS

Arranged by J. Mercer

With your right hand you play double notes, and with your left hand you play dotted half notes. The time signature is 3/4, so each dotted half note will sound one full measure.

## 71. BELLS ARE RINGING

Arranged by J. Mercer

In the 5th measure move your left hand to the right, and only in the 13th measure return it to its original position. Try! This piece trains the 4th and 5th fingers of both hands well.

## 72. JINGLE BELLS
### American New Year's Song

Arranged by J. Mercer

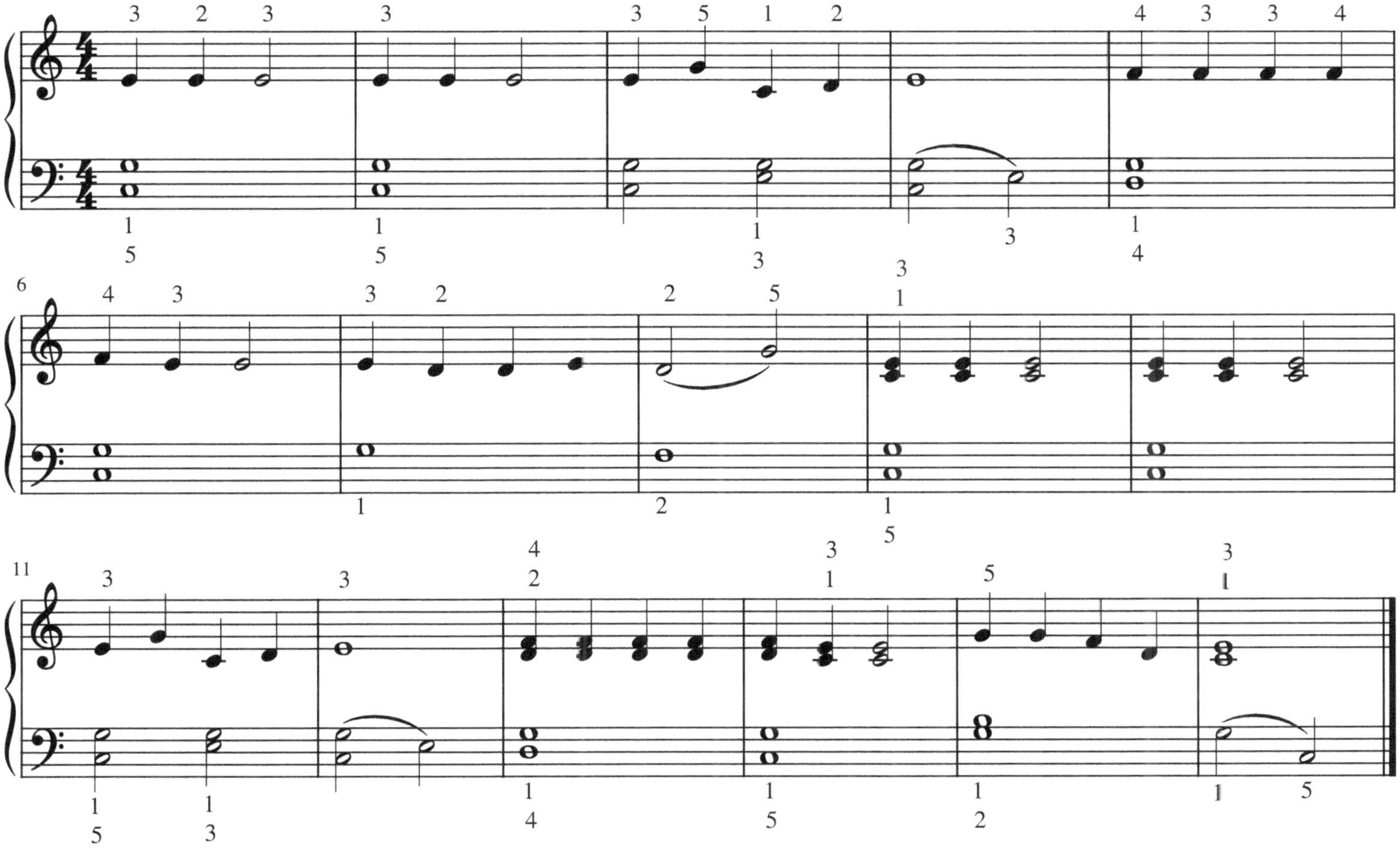

# LEARN TO CROSS YOUR FINGERS

To play new pieces correctly and smoothly, you must learn to cross your second finger over your first finger while playing, crossing these two fingers. Look at how the pianist crosses his 2nd finger over his 1st finger in these pictures.

| Here the fingers are in the normal position | Here the 2nd finger of the right hand position is transferred over the 1st | Here the 2nd finger of the left hand is transferred over the 1st |
|---|---|---|
|  |  |  |

Hold the fingers of your left hand as shown in the picture. Play these exercises as many times as you can until you learn to smoothly move the 2nd finger over the 1st and smoothly - without tension and without jerks - press the desired key with the 2nd finger.

Play these exercises slowly at first, and then increase the tempo and speed of the count as soon as you can. But only gradually! The most important thing: when moving your fingers, the hand should not rotate from side to side following the fingers. The arm and hand are in their normal position. The fingers themselves do all the work.

## 73. DANCE "THROUGH THE FINGER"

**Moderately**

Arranged by J. Mercer

In the 1st measure there is a note that is not on the right side of the keyboard and is not in the sound row of the First and Second octaves. But this note is familiar to you. Here it is in a separate drawing. You first played it in piece N° 37 "In the Forest". This key was located immediately to the left of the middle C key, and you pressed it with the 5th finger of your left hand. Now you already know that it was the note B of the Small octave from the left side of the keyboard, which is written on the lower staff above the 5th line - as in this drawing. Then it turns out that the same note is written differently? Why?

Because sometimes some notes of the Minor Octave need to be played not with the left hand, but with the right hand. And then the notes from the lower staff move to the additional lines of the upper staff, so that you play them with your right hand. Everything works out as shown in the picture.

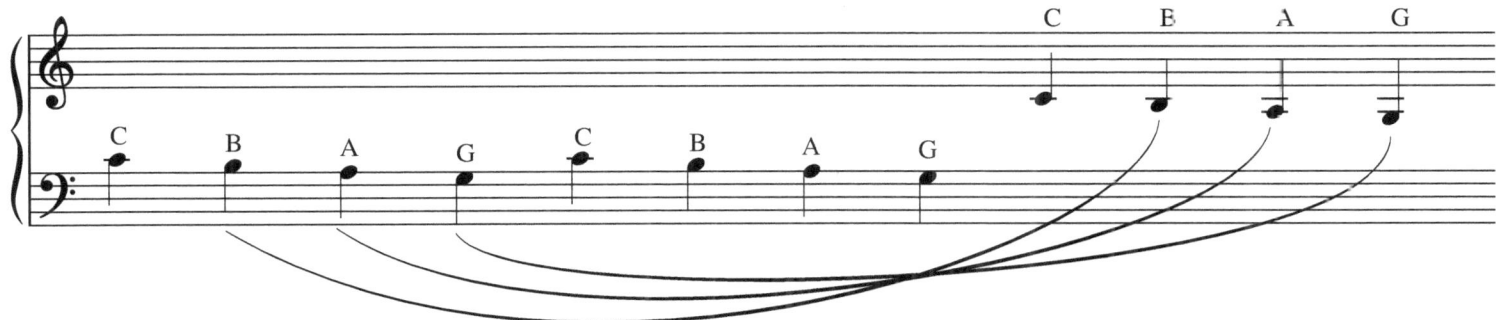

On the lower staff, A of the minor octave is on the 5th line, and G between the 5th and 4th. On the upper staff, the same note A goes to the lower 2nd additional line, and G - under the 2nd additional line. The note B of the minor octave is written on the upper staff under the lower 1st additional line.

In the last 4th measure of the piece "Dance "over the finger"" you see the note B of the Small octave again, but it has returned to its place - above the 5th line of the lower staff. It has returned because in this measure it is convenient to play it with the left hand, not the right. Play this note with the 1st finger.

In the 1st measure, transfer the 2nd finger of the right hand over the 1st to play the note B of the Small octave with this finger. In the 3rd measure, transfer the 2nd finger of the left hand over the 1st to play the note A of the Small octave. Do the transfer of fingers very smoothly, because these two measures must be played legato.

Simultaneously with the transfer of the 2nd finger to one side and then to the other, you must smoothly "step" from finger to finger.

The piece ends with a repeat sign (REPRISE) 𝄇. Therefore, you must repeat the piece from beginning to end. It will be good for your fingers to repeat it as often as possible.

## 74. THE OLD FARMER
### American song

Arranged by J. Mercer

**Moderately**

77

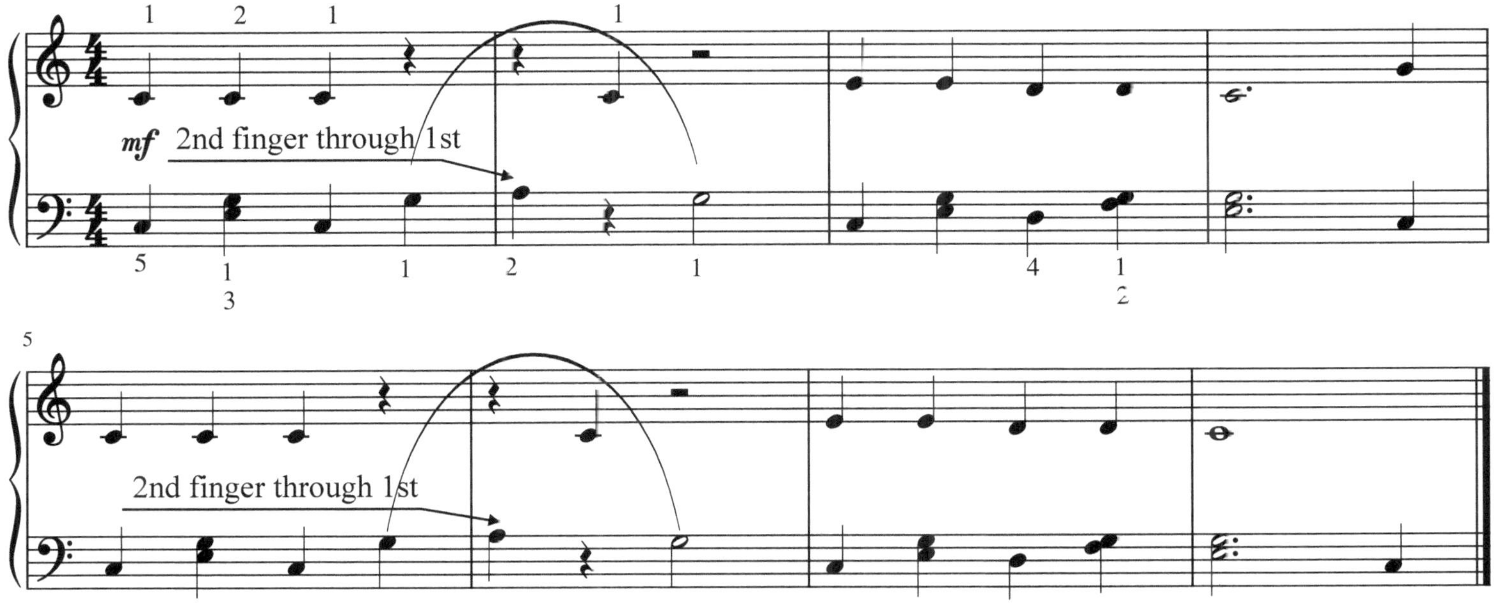

Start playing legato in the 1st measure with the 1st finger of the left hand, continue in the 2nd measure with the 2nd finger, then with the 1st finger of the right hand and finish also in the 2nd measure with the 1st finger of the left hand.

While playing legato, at the same time in the 2nd and 6th measures move the 2nd finger of the left hand over the 1st finger in one direction and in the other.

In the 1st and 5th measures, it is better to press the same C key with different fingers.

## 75. GOOD MOOD

**Joyfully**

Arranged by J. Mercer

Learn the first part of the piece first, then the second. And only then play both parts together. The fingerings are marked in the notes. Usually one part of the piece is separated from the other in the notes by two thin lines: ‖.

## 76. CATCH UP
### French song

Arranged by J. Mercer

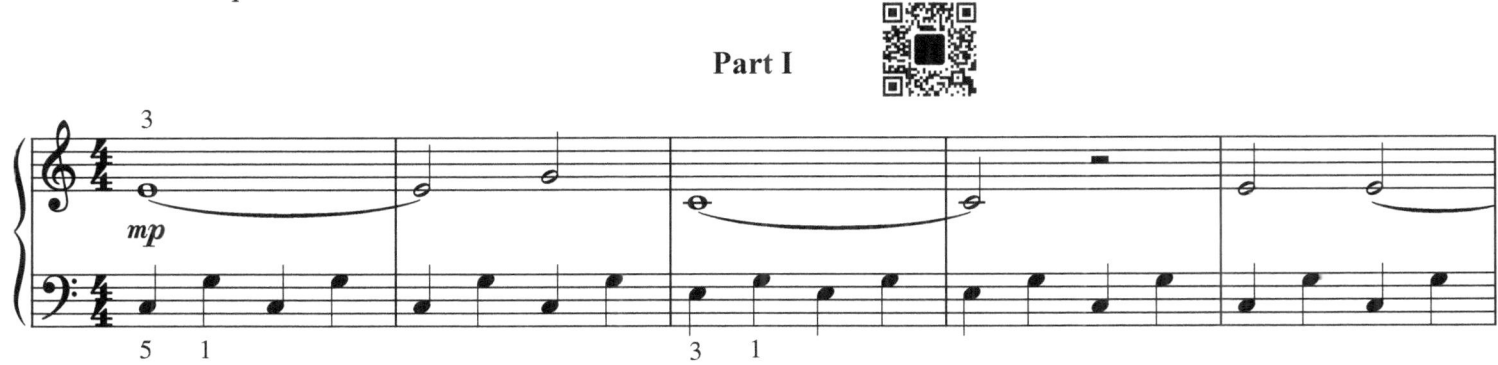

In the 5th, 6th, 7th, 13th and 14th measures, play the note B of the minor octave with the 1st finger of the right hand. In the 4th measure, play the same note B of the minor octave (this is the top note in the double half note) with the 1st finger of the left hand.

## 77. SPRING SONG OF THE NAVAJO INDIANS

A very rare and beautiful piece, one of the songs of the American Indians Navajo. This is a very famous tribe, but their "Spring Song" has never been heard in our country. Do you want to hear it first? Then first analyse the notes of this piece.

**Part I**

**Part II**

On the upper staff, the ligature unites all the measures standing next to each other: the 1st measure is united with the 2nd, the 3rd measure - with the 4th, the 5th - with the 6th, and so on until the very end of the piece.

*Pay attention to the main thing:* in many cases, the ligature connects two identical notes standing next to each other. For example, in the 1st and 2nd measures, the ligature connects two identical notes E, standing next to each other, as shown in the picture. When the ligature sign is between two IDENTICAL notes, they no longer say that the ligature unites, but they say that the ligature CONNECTS the notes, because it connects them into one common note with one common duration. The second note is not played separately. It turns out that the note E will sound continuously for four beats in the 1st measure and two more beats in the 2nd measure. In total, the note E will sound continuously for six beats. The note C in the 3rd and 4th measures will also sound for six beats. But the note E in the 5th and 6th measures will sound for four beats, because the ligament connects two half notes - two polys for each note.

It turns out that the ligament sign serves not only to combine several notes that need to be played legato. This sign also serves to increase the duration of any notes. Therefore, the duration of notes can be increased in two ways: with the help of a dot, which is placed to the right of the note ♩., or with the help of a slur ⌣ .

For example you can "make" a note sound for three beats in a row like this:

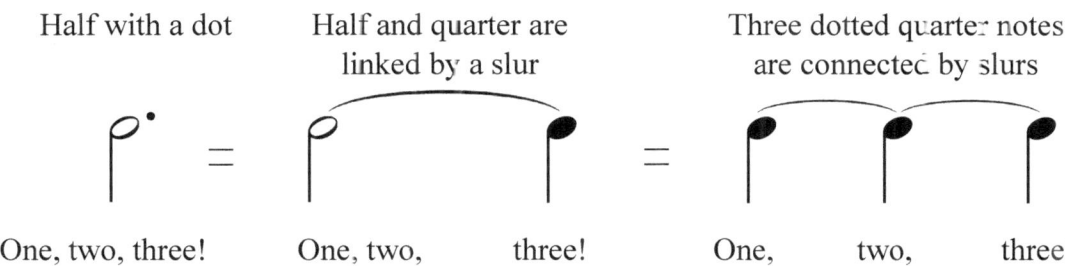

| Half with a dot | Half and quarter are linked by a slur | Three dotted quarter notes are connected by slurs |
|---|---|---|

One, two, three!     One, two, three!     One, two, three!

Determine for yourself how many beats the note D should sound in the 11th and 12th measures. Correct! The note D should sound continuously for five beats. Remember: if one lick or several slurs connect two or more identical notes standing next to each other, then only the first note is played. And this first note "takes" the durations of all the other notes, and sounds without interruption, "one for two" or "one for all".

Examine again in the 1st and 2nd measures the two notes E, connected by a slur into one common "long" note. This note sounds a full four beats in the 1st measure, then takes over the first two beats in the 2nd measure, and sounds six beats in a row.

Count out loud this "long" note E: "One, two, three, four, one, two!" See what happened to the accent in the 2nd measure? The 1st measure has a strong beat, but the 2nd measure has lost its strong beat because it lost the accent on the second count "one". This happens not only in the 2nd measure, but also in the 4th, 6th, 8th and others. And then the melody gets a new complex and very beautiful rhythm.

One,
Two,
Three,
Four!

One,
Two!

With your left hand, play the accompaniment evenly with quarter notes, which convey the rhythm of Indian drums.

And now you must learn to move the third finger over the first, crossing these two fingers, right while playing. Look how in these pictures the pianist moves the 3rd finger of the right hand over the 1st finger.

| **Fingers in normal position** | **The third finger is carried over the first** |
|---|---|

Hold the fingers of your right hand as shown in the pictures. Play these exercises as many times as you can until you learn to smoothly move the 3rd finger over the 1st, and smoothly - without tension and without jerks - press the desired key with the 3rd finger.

Play these exercises slowly at first, and then increase the tempo and counting speed as soon as you can. But only gradually! The most important thing: when moving your fingers, the hand should not rotate from side to side following the fingers. The arm and hand are in their usual position. The fingers themselves do all the work. And the hand makes only a very light and smooth lateral movement towards the finger that is being moved.

*Note:* the fingers move DIFFERENTLY in one direction and in the other: in one direction - the 1st finger seems to be "inserted" under the 3rd, and in the other direction - the 3rd finger crosses the 1st finger.

Play these exercises energetically, and not with a "sluggish" hand. When playing, do not forget about the accent on the first strong beat, and even emphasise it.

And in these pictures, the pianist moves the 3rd finger of the left hand over the 1st finger.

| **Fingers in normal position** | **The third finger is transferred over the first** |
|---|---|

Hold the fingers of your left hand as shown in the pictures. Practice these exercises in exactly the same way as the exercises for the fingers of your right hand.

## 78. STARS IN SPACE
### French melody

Arranged by J. Mercer

3rd finger transfer

3rd finger transfer

# LEARN TO PLAY SCALES

For speed and agility of fingers, you need to play special parts of the scale, which are called "scales". A scale is a "company" of sounds that are very friendly, always follow each other and make up a scale. The first and simplest is the C major scale. It begins and ends with the note C, and sounds cheerful, energetic, or, as musicians say, "major".

Pianists all over the world play scales to train their fingers. Now you too will play the C major scale and learn to quickly and easily move your fingers.

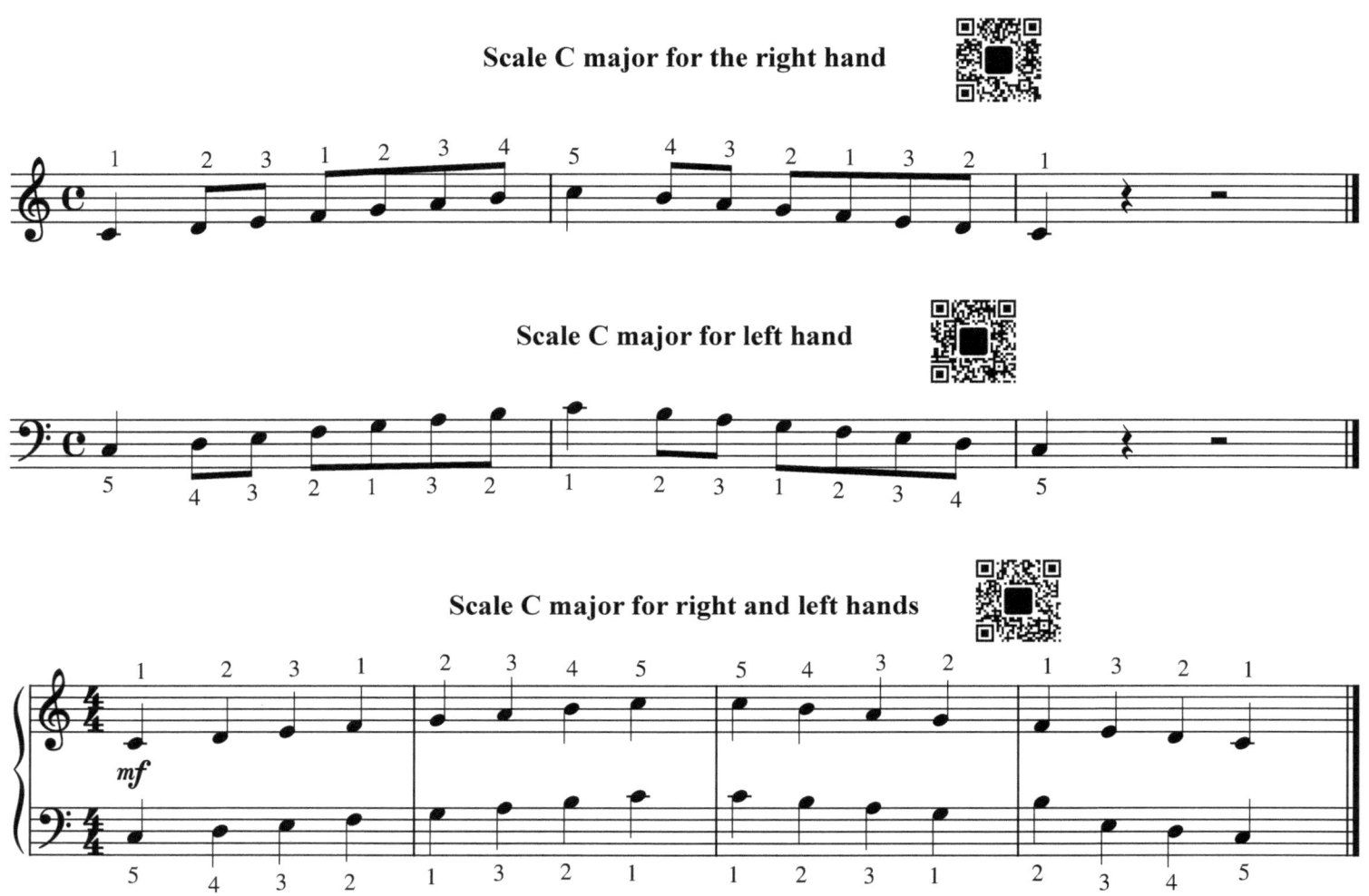

To play scales correctly and with benefit for your fingers, remember six main rules:
- play the scale first with your right hand, then with your left, and then with both hands at once;
- after you learn the scale, gradually increase the tempo of the game every day;
- count out loud - then try to count silently. If everything goes well, gradually increase the tempo of the game as much as you can. But only gradually!
- play the scale EVENLY. Gradually achieve that the transfer and placement of fingers become completely imperceptible to the ear;
- press the keys with the same average force, so that all notes of the scale sound with the same volume;
- constantly monitor the CORRECT position of your hands and fingers on the keys. Even if you play the scale very quickly, and your hand rotates from side to side or "falls" towards the 5th finger, and the fingers themselves are not ROUNDED, but flat, "splayed out" or, on the contrary, "stick together", then such "fast" playing will do more harm than good.

# 79. ESCALATOR

Arranged by J. Mercer

**Calmly**

In the 3rd and 4th measures on the upper staff, two adjacent G notes are tied by a tie.
Therefore, the G note will sound for five quarter notes in total - one quarter in the 3rd measure and four quarters in the 4th measure. Count in advance how many quarter notes the other "tied" notes will sound.

In the 6th measure on the lower staff, under the G note of the Minor Octave, there are two numbers "4-1". But you cannot press this key with two fingers at once - the 4th and 1st. These numbers tell you that while the G note will sound for as many as 5 quarter notes, you must, without releasing this key, change your 4th finger to the 1st right on it, in order to prepare the 1st finger in advance for the double note E - G, which is in the next 8th measure.

# LEARN TO PLAY CHORDS ON THE WHITE KEYS

When more than two different sounds sound at the same time, musicians say - "a chord sounds". The Latin word "accordo" means - "I harmonise", so the sounds in a chord sound in harmony, consonant with each other. Most often in music there are chords of three sounds, which are called TRIADS. But any three sounds cannot form a triad - for this, specially selected sounds are needed. Only musicians do not say - "pick up sobriety", they say - "build a triad".

Triads are built from any note of the octave scale. Here, seven triads are built without using black keys from all seven main sounds of the octave: C, D, E, F, G, A, B.

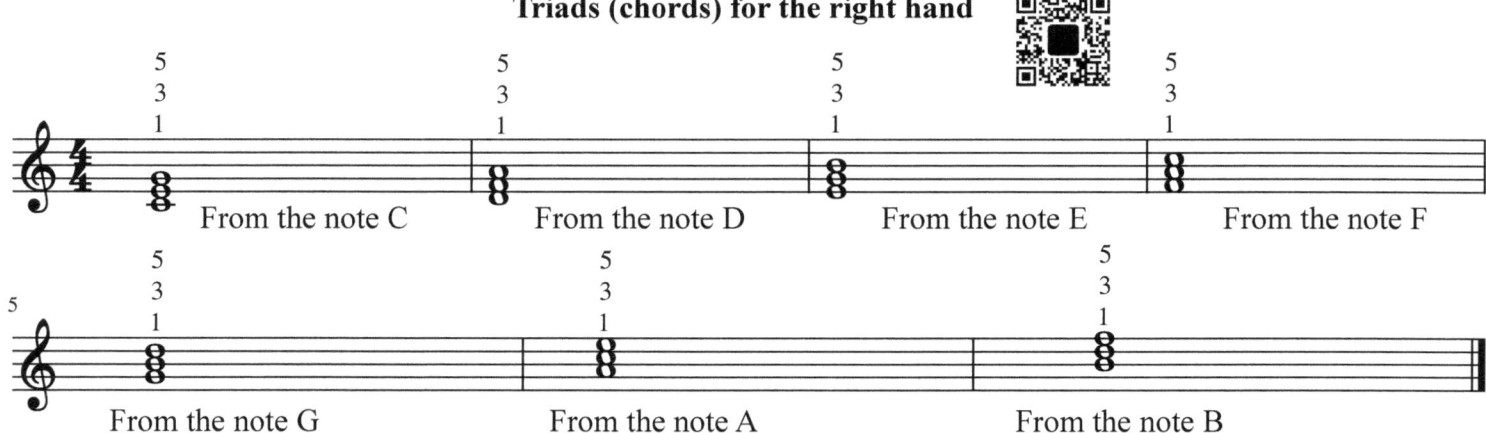

Play these triads exactly as you played the double notes. With three rounded fingers, press three keys at once so that all three notes start and stop sounding AT THE SAME TIME, and none of them breaks ahead or lags behind the other two. The numbers of the three fingers are indicated next to each note of the triad.

Play the triads as many times as necessary until they start to sound together and in harmony.

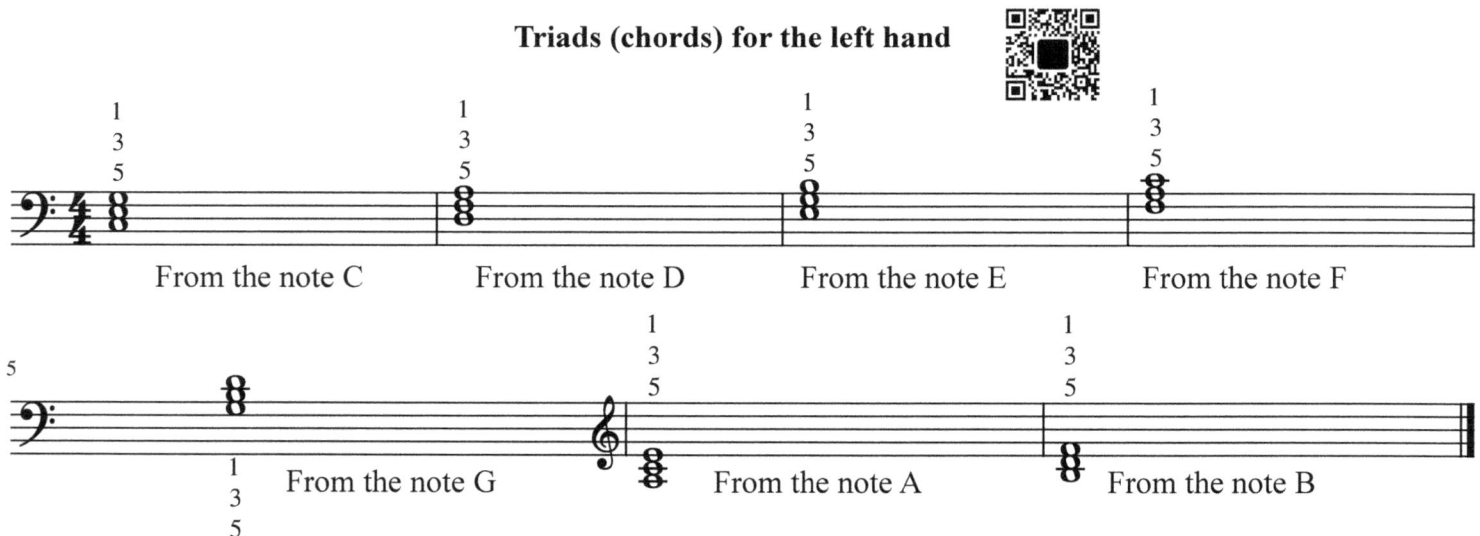

Play these triads with three fingers of your left hand.

Before the 6th measure, the Treble Clef has appeared on the lower staff instead of the Bass Clef. This technique is used when the left hand must play some notes on the right side of the keyboard. Therefore, in the 6th and 7th measures, your left hand will press the C, D, E, F keys of the First Octave.

You already know how notes "move" from one staff to another. This picture shows how it happens again.

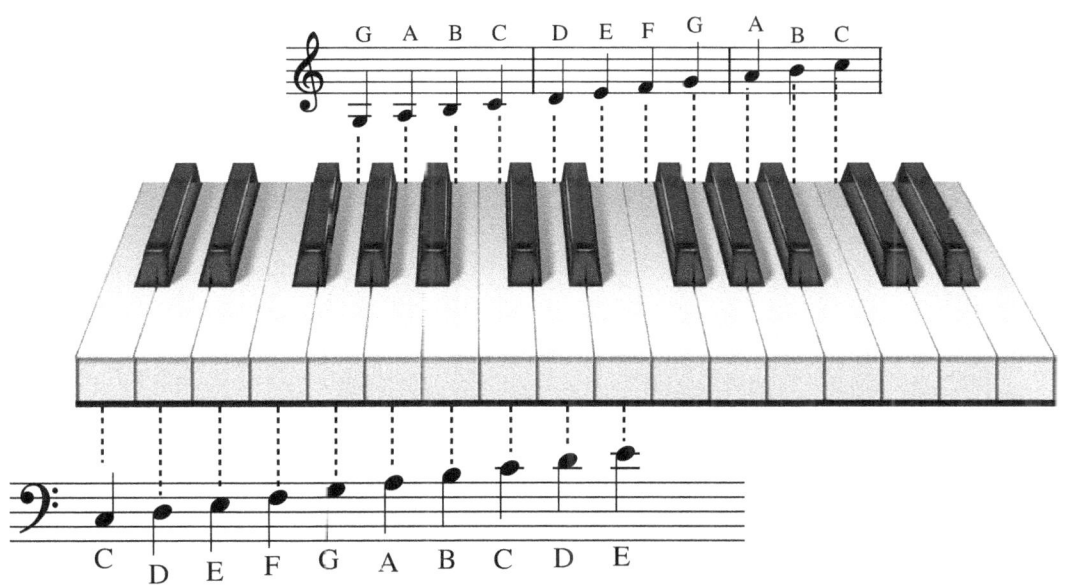

## 80. THERE ARE EIGHT CHORDS IN THE RIGHT HAND

Arranged by J. Mercer

**Slowly**

Here the melody is played by the left hand, the accompaniment by the right. Each measure repeats the same musical phrase, which each time "moves" across the keyboard one white key to the right.

# 81. THERE ARE EIGHT CHORDS IN THE LEFT HAND

Arranged by J. Mercer

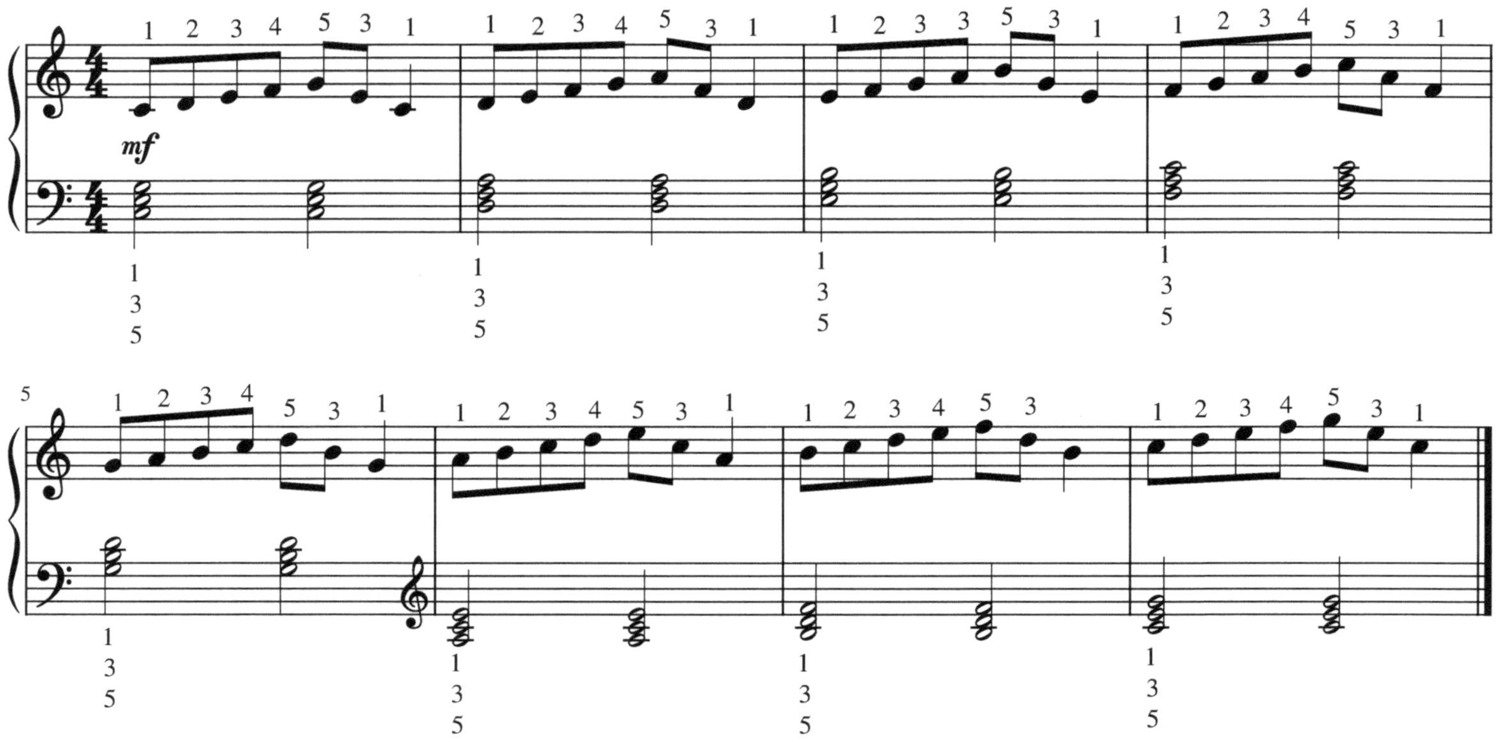

Here the melody is played by the right hand, the accompaniment by the left.

# 82. DANCE OF AFRICAN SORCERERS

Arranged by J. Mercer

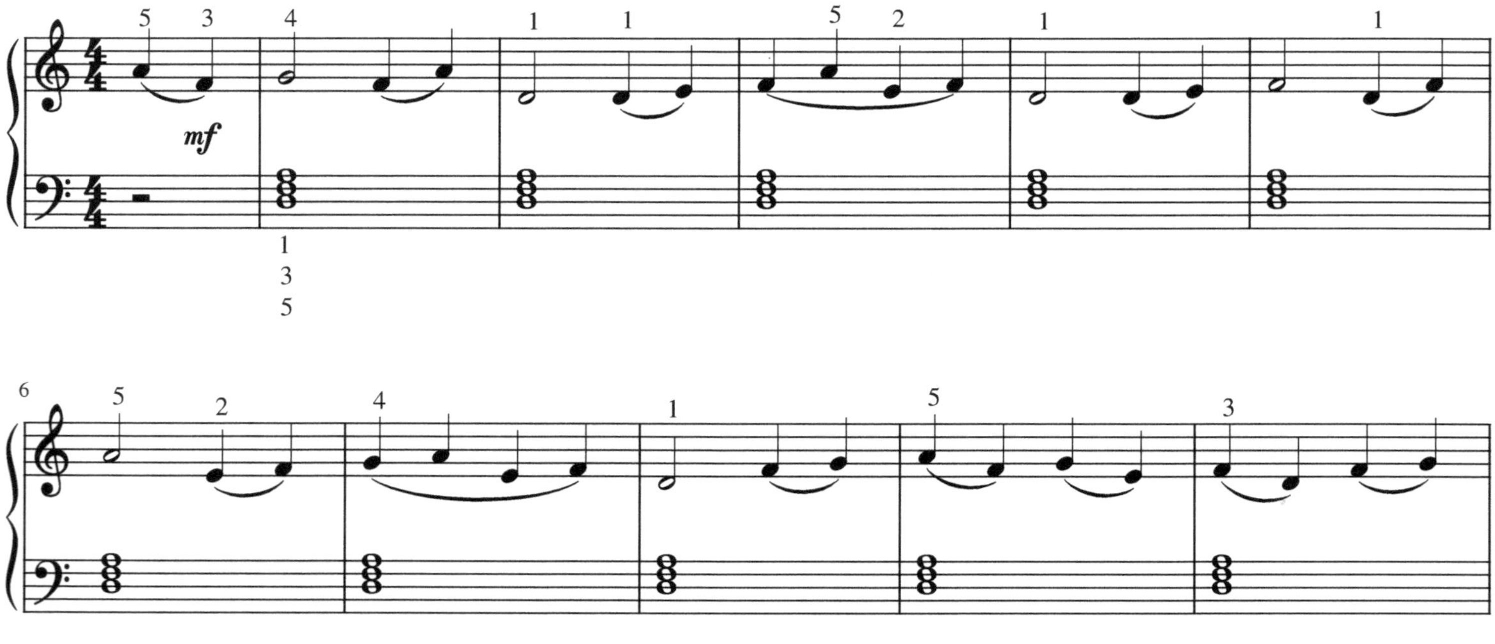

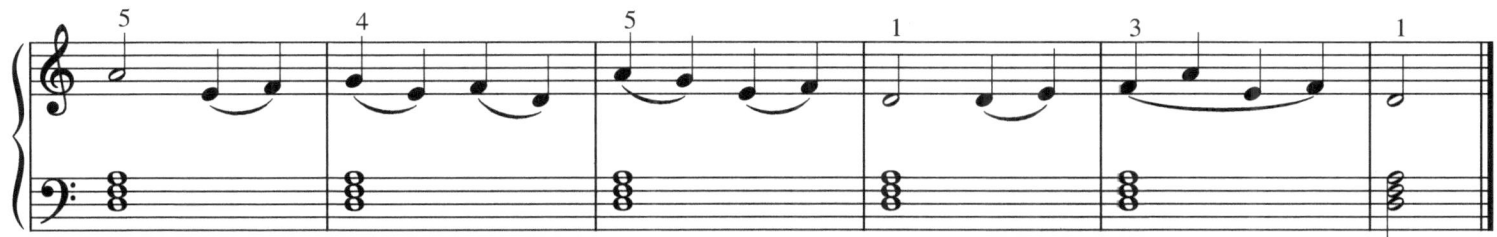

The measure of this piece is four quarter notes. But in the 1st measure there are only two quarter notes on the upper staff, and a half rest on the lower staff.

It turns out that the 1st measure is INCOMPLETE - it lacks two more quarter notes. This is done so that the melody begins immediately with the third quarter of the 1st measure, which is not as strong as the first quarter. Therefore, you should not make an accent in the 1st measure. Such an incomplete 1st measure is called - BEAT. Musicians say that the piece begins with the pickup.

But an incomplete pickup, as a rule, is completely replenished by the last measure. In the last incomplete 17th measure of the piece there is only one half note. And then the total duration of the pickup and the last incomplete measure is four quarter notes.

Your right hand should take a new position. Move your hand one white key to the right so that your 1st finger is above the D key. Watch the new placement of your fingers on the keys. Play the same chords-triads evenly with your left hand, which should sound like a large African drum.

# FIGURE OUT HOW THE CHORDS ARE "ARRANGED" (TRIADS)

All the pieces you played before sounded "major" - cheerful, fun and energetic. But when you learned the last piece - "Dance of the African Sorcerers", then, of course, you felt "by ear" that this piece had a "company" of notes that sounded completely different from the MAJOR. It does not sound cheerful, and not cheerful, and not energetic. Such a joyless "company" of notes is called minor or simply MINOR. The word "minor" comes from the Latin words "lesser" and "soft". So it turns out that in a minor "company" all the notes have less cheerfulness, less firmness and fun. However, the melody of the piece "Dance of the African Sorcerers" sounds harmonious and harmonious.

Any song or melody will sound harmonious and harmonious if all its sounds, to a single one, are part of one common "company". A musical "company" in which musical sounds are friendly and in harmony with each other is called a "musical SCALE". There are two such "companies" in music: a major musical SCALE (or simply MAJOR) and a minor musical SCALE (or simply MINOR). Therefore, chords-triads can be either major or minor. Figure out how they are "arranged" and what is the difference between them.

You have already figured out earlier how an octave is "arranged", and learned that between the main musical sounds: C, D, E, F, G, A, B, there are INTERVALS (gaps) of different pitches. Let's compare the pattern of the octave INTERVALS with the first two triads built from the note C and from the note D.

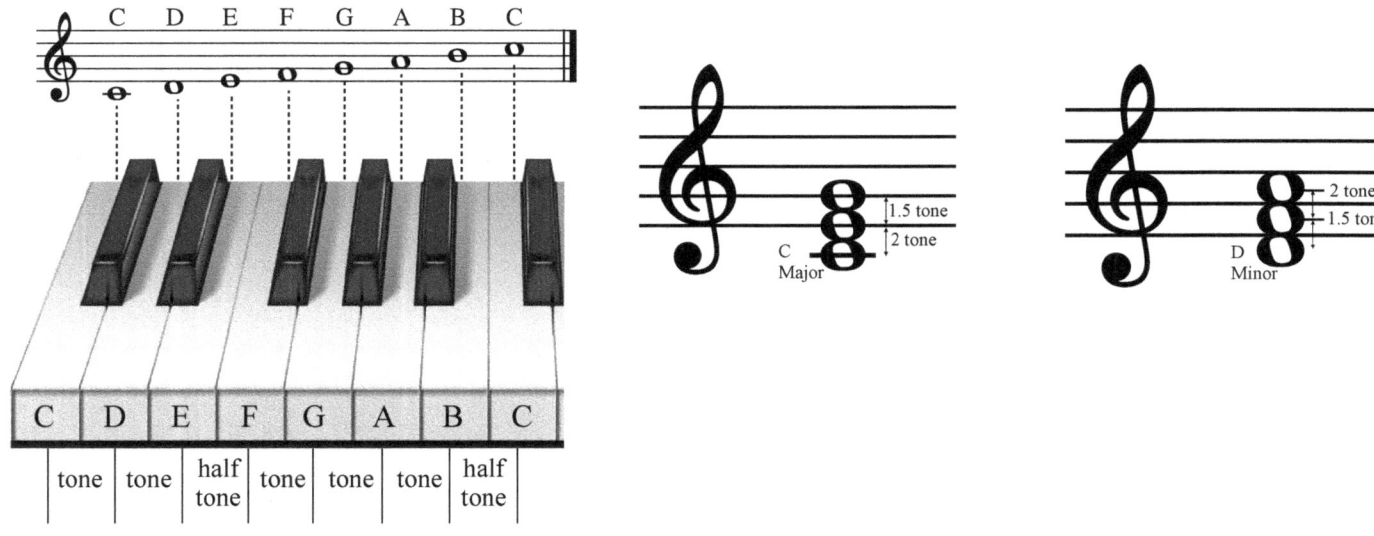

Each of these two triads covers FIVE octave steps.

Triad from C: C — (d) — E — (f) — G
            I     II    III   IV    V

Triad from D: D — (e) — F — (g) — A
            I     II    III   IV    V

But these two triads are "arranged" differently. In a triad from the note C, the interval between the I and III degrees is 2 tones, and between the III and V degrees - 1.5 tones. But in a triad from the note D, everything is the other way around: the interval between the I and III degrees is 1.5 tones, and between the III and V degrees - 2 tones. All other triads are constructed in one of these two ways.

Triads that are constructed like a triad from the note C are called major. These triads sound cheerful, joyful, energetic, bright.

Triads that are constructed like a triad from the note D are called minor. They sound gentle, soft, sad, and sometimes mysterious and even ominous, as, for example, in the last piece "The Dance of the Sorcerers".

**For the curious!** It is impossible to explain why the sound of triads changes so unexpectedly, if they only swap intervals of 1.5 and 2 tones. This is a mystery, or rather, a law of nature associated with human perception of different sounds. Using the drawing and the piano keyboard, independently determine which of the remaining five chords-triads are major and which are minor.

## 83. HANUKKAH
### Jewish song-dance

Arranged by J. Mercer

**Joyfully**

## LEARN TO PLAY ARPEGGIO

### 84. GOOD MOOD

Arranged by J. Mercer

**Lively**

Look at the notes of the piece you have already played (N° 75). Pay attention to the notes of the 1st measure C, E, G and G, E, C. And also to the notes of the 2nd measure - B, D, F. These notes together can form two triads. But now you need to play not a triad, but one note after another. If you play the notes of a triad one after another, they turn into an ARPEGGIO of this triad. The Italian word "arpeggio" means "like a harp". Therefore, you should pluck the keys and sounds of the sober one after another, like strings stretched on a harp or a guitar.

Learn and play an arpeggio, which is formed from a triad built from the note C. Imagine that the triad is a beautiful rose. Then the arpeggio is its petals. Learn to unfold the "petals" of this "rose".

**Arpeggio from a triad built from the note C**

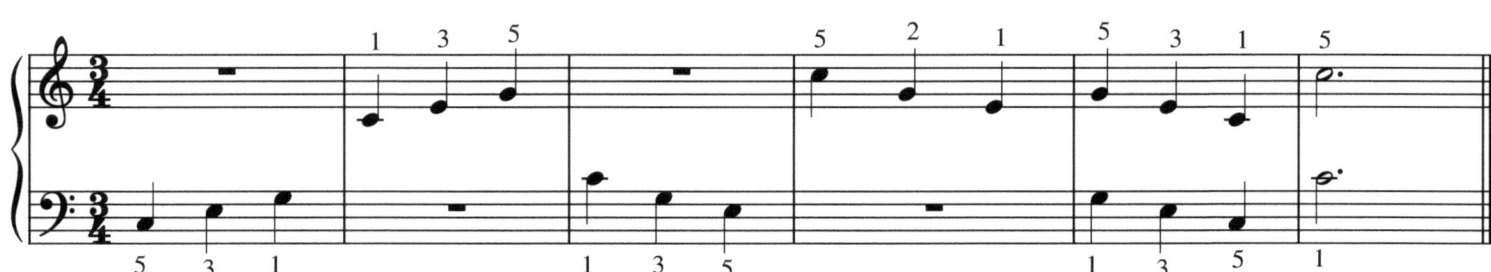

Now learn and play the piece "Good Mood". The melody is familiar to you - you have already played it. But now it will sound different. With your right hand, "unfold the rose" in the 1st, 3rd and 9th measures. With your left hand, "unfold the rose" in the 1st, 2nd, 3rd, 4th, 5th, 7th, 8th, 9th and 11th measures. The melody sounds especially beautiful when you "unfold the rose" with both hands in the 1st, 3rd and 9th measures.

Before playing a new piece, you need to get acquainted with a new playing technique called "crossing your hands". This means that right during the game, your hands will be in a crossed position for some time - one hand above the other. Look at this picture and you will understand yourself why it is necessary. The pianist's left hand is above the right hand and helps it play on the right part of the keyboard. The main thing here is not to "twitch" your hands and move your hand QUIETLY and SMOOTHLY.

## 85. PLAYING CLASSICS

Arranged by J. Mercer

**Movably**

The dotted line indicates that in the 7th measure after the double note F-G, you need to move your left hand over your right and with the 2nd finger of your left hand play the note E of the Second Octave in the 8th last measure.

92

# 86. PYRAMID

Arranged by J. Mercer

On the upper staff in the 2nd, 6th, 18th and 22nd measures play the note A with the 2nd finger of the left hand. Smoothly transfer the left hand and cross it over the right hand. In the last measure play the note C of the Second Octave with the left hand.

# LEARN TO PLAY THE STACCATO WAY

Now you must learn another way of playing the piano, which is called STACCATO. The Italian word "staccato" means "abruptly". This word does not go well with the word "legato", because "legato" refers to smooth and drawn-out sounds, while "staccato" is the opposite - it requires short and abrupt sounds. When the piano is played the "staccato" way, it sounds special - as if rain is drumming on a window or tram wheels are clattering on the rails. To get such a short and abrupt sound, you must press the key sharply and release it even faster than you pressed it. Then the "hammer" will sharply hit the string and immediately bounce off it. The string will "scream" briefly and immediately fall silent. Short and sharp strokes will produce short and abrupt sounds, because the sounds will "march" one after another with small breaks or pauses.

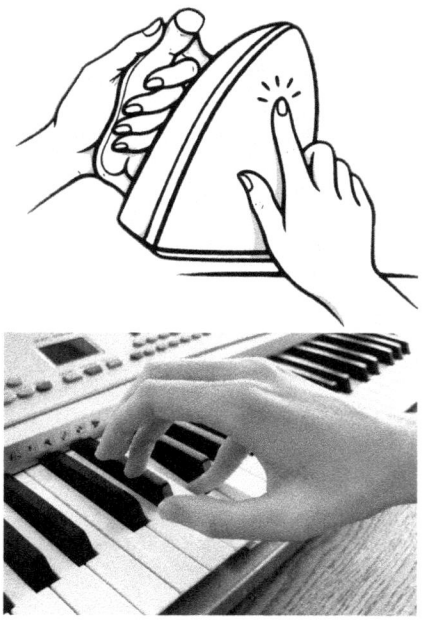

These pauses are not indicated in any way in the notes, but if there is a dot UNDER or ABOVE the note, as in this picture, it means that the note should be played staccato. Imagine that you are not just pressing a key with your finger, but touching a very hot iron. Your finger hurts, and you immediately pull it away. And then you continue to press the keys so quickly that you do not have time to burn yourself, as shown in the picture.

When playing staccato, you can use your hand to help your finger "bounce" off the key a little faster. Look how in this picture the pianist helps his fingers play staccato with his whole hand. Just don't swing your hand up and down too much, as if you were chopping greens with a knife in the kitchen. Your finger and hand movements should be fast, but at the same time smooth, light and economical. Economical means not sweeping and not tense. You can help your fingers play staccato not only with your hand, but even with your hand. But the hand movements should not be very sharp and almost imperceptible.

Learn and play a new piece. It was written specifically so that you can quickly learn to play staccato.

## 87. BOUNCING BALL

Arranged by J. Mercer

At the very beginning, under the staff, there is the word Forte. This means that the piece should be played loudly. *Note:* the TEMPO of the play is always indicated ABOVE the staff, and the VOLUME of the sound is indicated BELOW the staff.

In this piece, all the notes with the "baton" pointing up, you play with your right hand. And all the notes with the "baton" lowered, you play with your left hand. In all the measures of the piece there are only quarter notes. But when you start playing staccato and sharply press and quickly release the keys, the quarter notes will not sound their full duration, but only at the moment of your strike on the key. Immediately after your quick strike, there will be a small pause, and the duration of the quarter note will be shortened. It is believed that staccato makes the quarter note shorter by about half. Everything turns out as shown in this

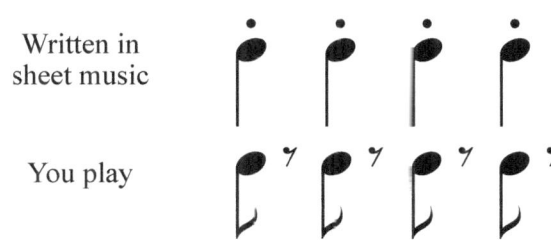

picture. You count and play quarter notes, and eighth rests sound. The ⅞ sign denotes a rest equal in duration to one eighth note, that is why it is called the EIGHTH rest. Like all other rests, you count eighth rests, but do not play them. *Remember the main thing:* playing "staccato", you shorten the sound of each note, but this should not in any way affect the EVENNESS of your counting and the THEME of your playing. The quarter note was a "quarter", and it remains so. You just "take away" from each note approximately half of its "legal" sound.

## 88. UKRAINIAN DANCE

Arranged by J. Mercer

**Joyfully**

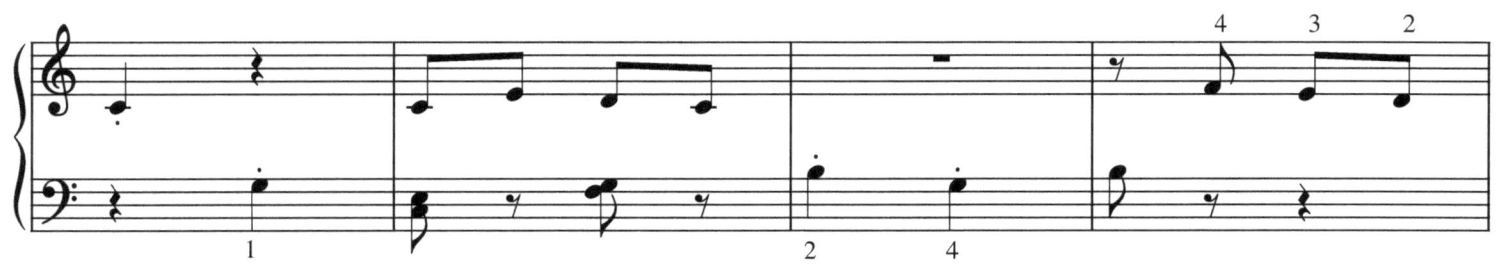

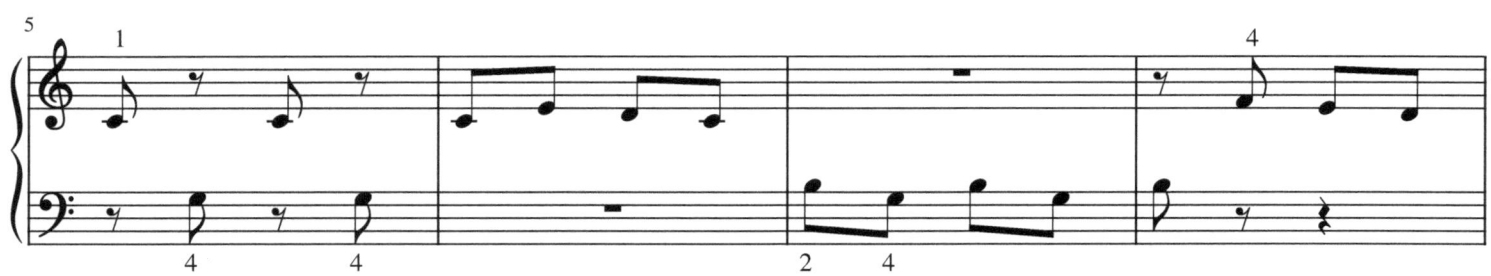

All quarter notes in this piece you play "staccato". Pay special attention to the eighth pauses. There are pause signs in every measure, but the melody of the dance is never interrupted. When one hand is not playing, the other must play. In the 9th measure there is the word "accelerating". This means that from this point until the end of the piece you must increase the tempo of your playing. Play this piece as cheerfully as possible, and then - gradually - as quickly as possible. The music of this dance should sound loud, cheerful and fly quickly, like a bird.

# LEARN TO PLAY PIECES ON WHITE AND BLACK KEYS

It's time to figure out why the black keys "march" on the keyboard in twos and even threes. A long time ago, back in Ancient Greece, musicians realised that music would be more beautiful and richer if there were more than seven sounds in an octave. Then they decided to divide each whole step of the musical "ladder" into two halves, so that between all the sounds of the octave there would be the same interval, equal to half a tone (half a "step"!). They did not touch the steps with a height of HALF A TONE. And to the middle of each of the five steps with a height of one TONE they "attached" one additional step, as in this picture.

These five additional "steps" are the five black keys that "march" in twos and threes. They simply cannot "march" in any other way. There is nowhere to insert an additional "step" between the white keys E and F, as well as between B and C. There is already a low "step" between them - only a half-tone. So it turned out that between all the sounds and keys of the octave - both white and black - the interval in pitch became the same and equal to half a tone.

Count how many semitones there are in an octave. That's right! Exactly as many as all the "steps" together with the additional ones - a total of twelve semitones. That's why they say that the interval of an octave is equal to six tones or twelve semitones.

Now you must learn to correctly call the black keys by name. These keys do not have their own names. The black key takes its name from one of the white keys between which it is located. Therefore, it turns out that each black key has not one, but two names.

Imagine that you climb up all twelve "steps" of the octave - both white and black. With each "step" the sounds become higher by half a tone, as in this picture.

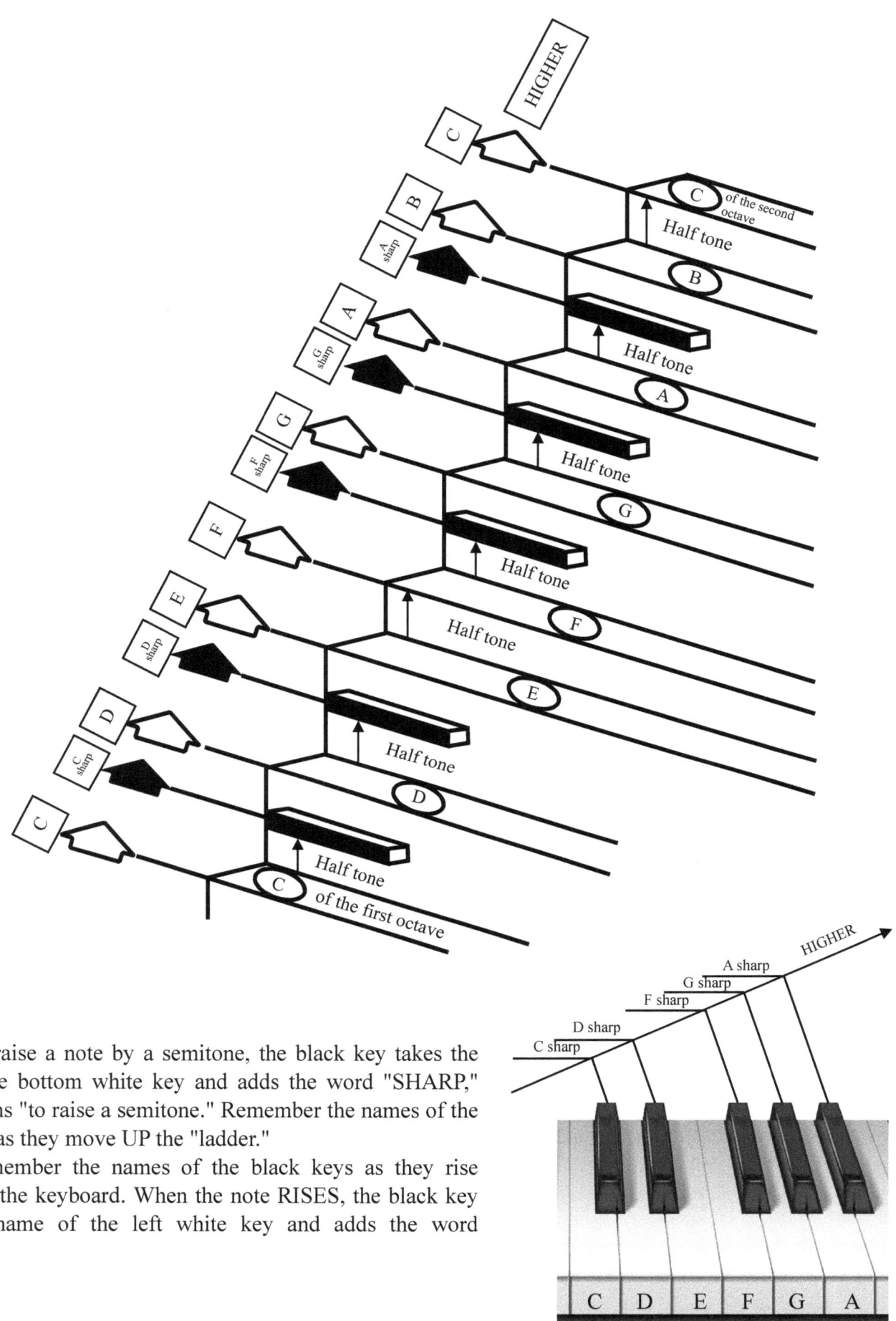

To raise a note by a semitone, the black key takes the name of the bottom white key and adds the word "SHARP," which means "to raise a semitone." Remember the names of the black keys as they move UP the "ladder."

Remember the names of the black keys as they rise directly on the keyboard. When the note RISES, the black key takes the name of the left white key and adds the word "SHARP."

Now imagine that you are going down all twelve "steps" of the octave - both white and black. With each "step" the sounds become lower by a semitone, as in this picture.

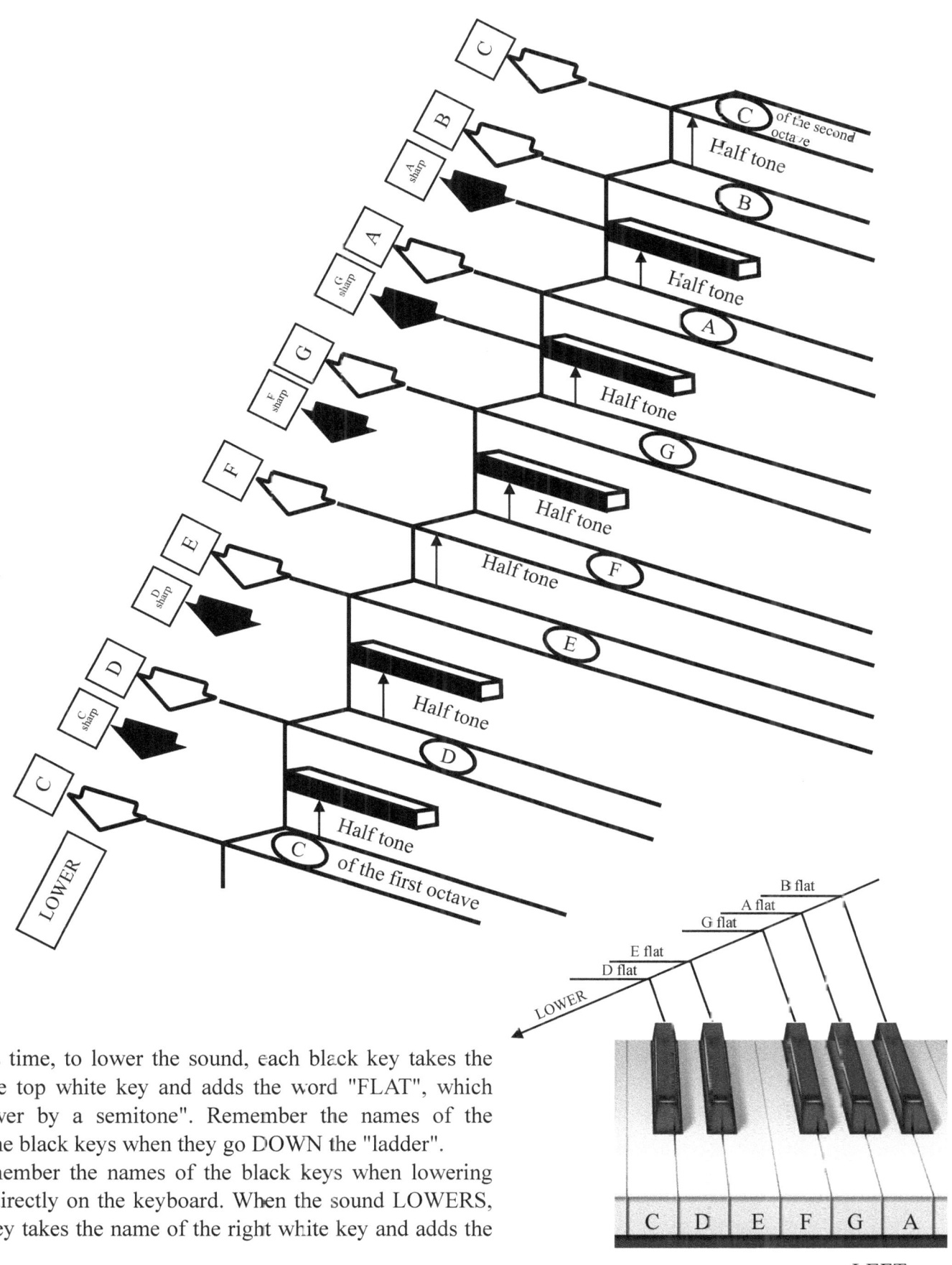

This time, to lower the sound, each black key takes the name of the top white key and adds the word "FLAT", which means "lower by a semitone". Remember the names of the sounds of the black keys when they go DOWN the "ladder".

Remember the names of the black keys when lowering the sound directly on the keyboard. When the sound LOWERS, the black key takes the name of the right white key and adds the word "flat".

# 89. "TIC-TAC-TOE"

**Part I**

Joyfully

Arranged by J. Mercer

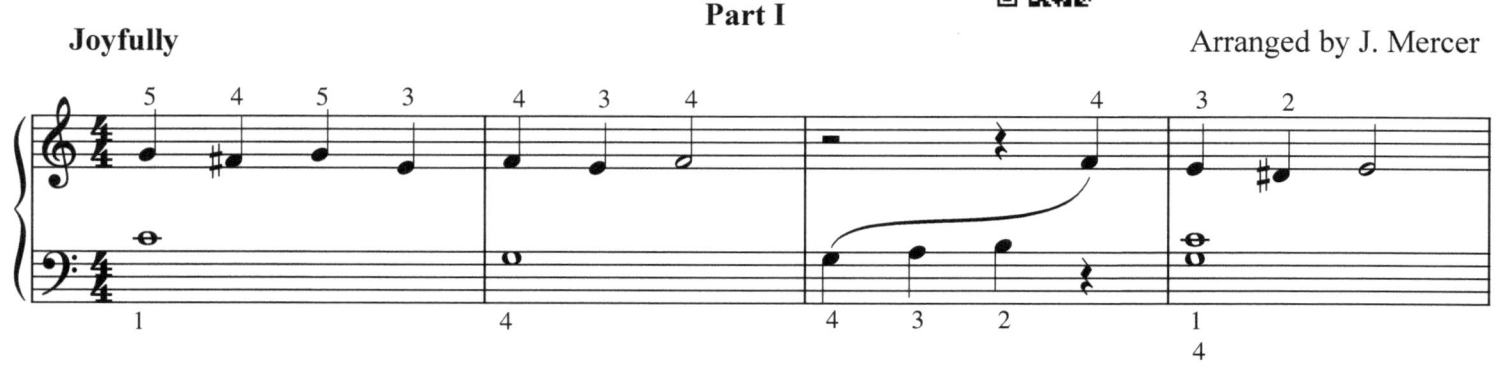

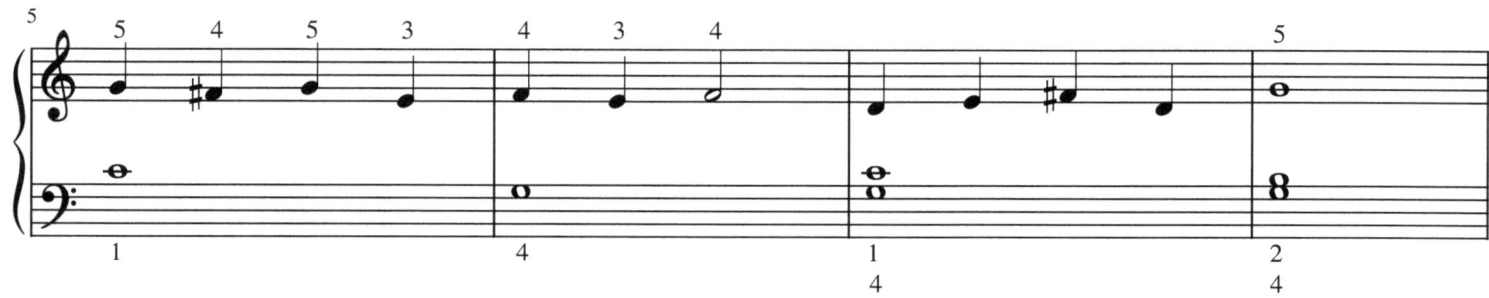

**Part II**

In the 1st measure, there is a ♯ sign before the F note. This sign is called a sharp. You are already familiar with the word sharp. It means that the note that has the sharp sign before it needs to be raised by half a tone.

It turns out that the white key F took a "day off", and instead of it the black key F-sharp lying to the right should work, which sounds a half tone higher. But in the 2nd measure the note F has already returned to its place. In the 4th measure the note D took a "day off", and instead of it the black key D-sharp will also work, as shown in this picture. The white keys F and D take "day off" in other measures as well: in the 5th, 7th, 9th, 12th and 13th. Instead of them you need to press the black keys lying to the right, and they will sound a half tone higher than the white keys F and D.

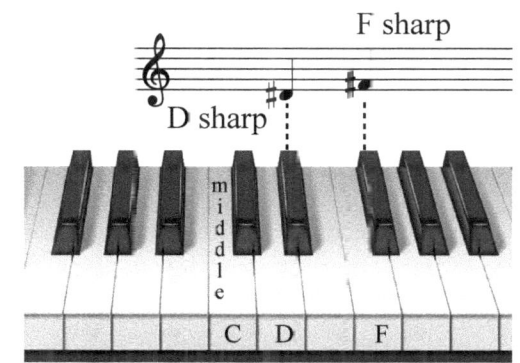

In the 13th measure on the lower staff above the note B there is a sign ♭. It is called "flat". You know this word too. It means that the note preceded by the "flat" sign must be lowered by half a tone.

It turns out that now the "off" note is the B of the Small Octave, and it is "replaced" by the note B-flat, which sounds half a tone lower. Therefore, you need to press the black key lying to the left of the note B, as shown in this picture. The "sharp" sign and the "flat" sign are active throughout the entire measure in which these signs are placed. But they cannot raise or lower notes in other - even neighbouring measures. Beyond the measure line of their own measure, the effect of these signs ends. You can assume that the "flat" or "sharp" signs, if they appear in any measure, have enough "power" only for this one measure.

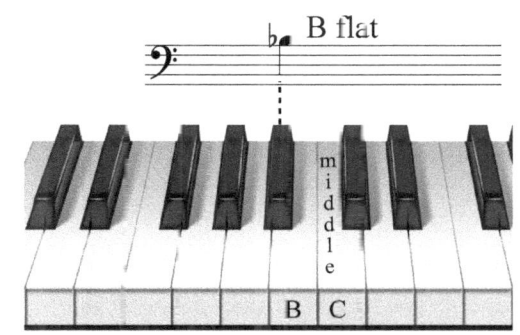

## 90. FAR OVER THE OCEAN
### Traditional Scottish song

Arranged by J. Mercer

**Slowly with feeling**

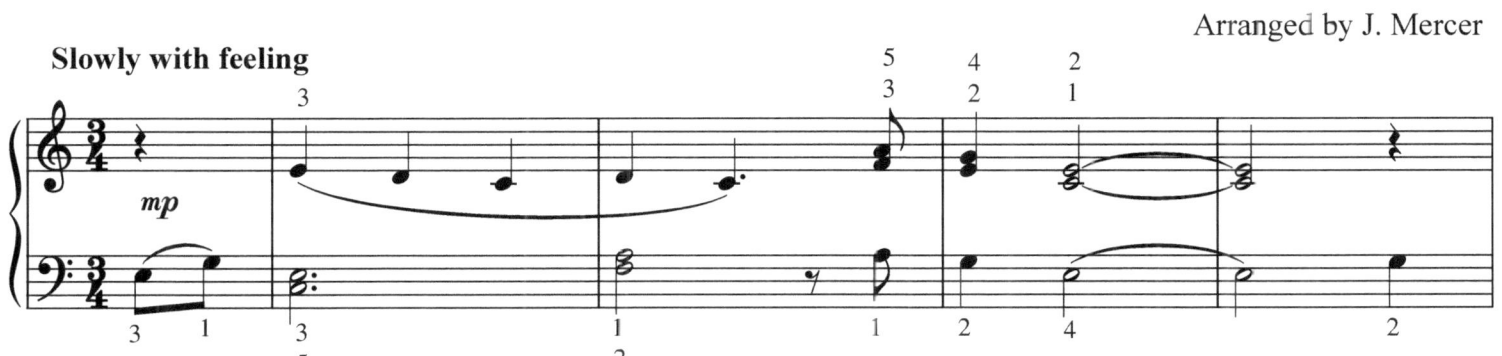

The sign ——————◁ means that you need to gradually increase the volume.

## 91. ELEVATOR TO THE EIFFEL TOWER

Arranged by J. Mercer

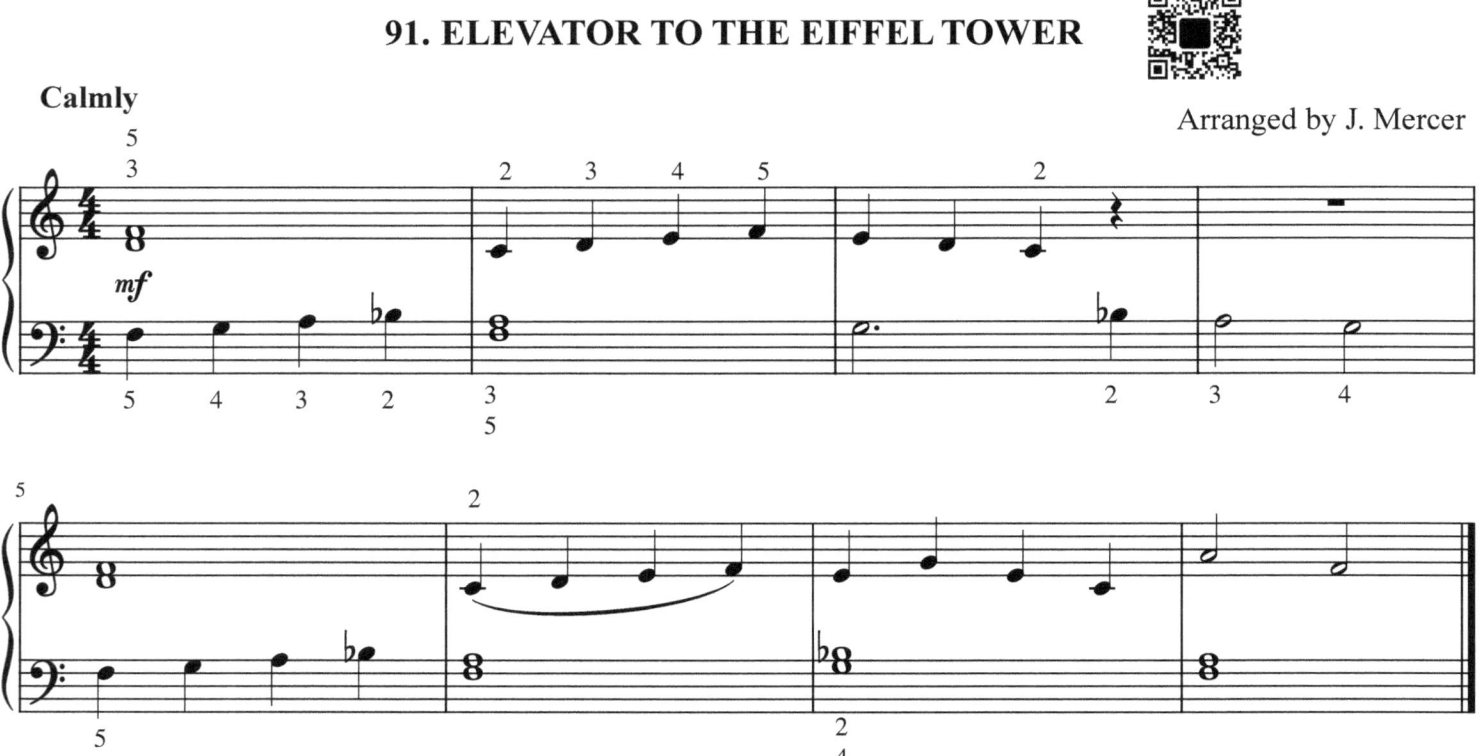

Play this piece with a new arrangement of fingers over the keys. Hide the 1st fingers under the palms, and place the remaining fingers over the keys so that the 5th fingers are ready to press the F keys of the First and Small Octaves. There is news for your left hand: the note B of the Small Octave has taken a "day off", and instead you will play the note B-flat. Press the black key with the 2nd finger.

# LEARN TO PLAY IN F MAJOR POSITION

Now you will become familiar with a new position of the fingers on the keys or, as pianists say, a new "hand position". Distribute your fingers over the keys of the First and Small octaves as shown in the picture. Touch the keys with your fingertips. The 2nd finger of the left hand and the 4th finger of the right hand touch the black keys.

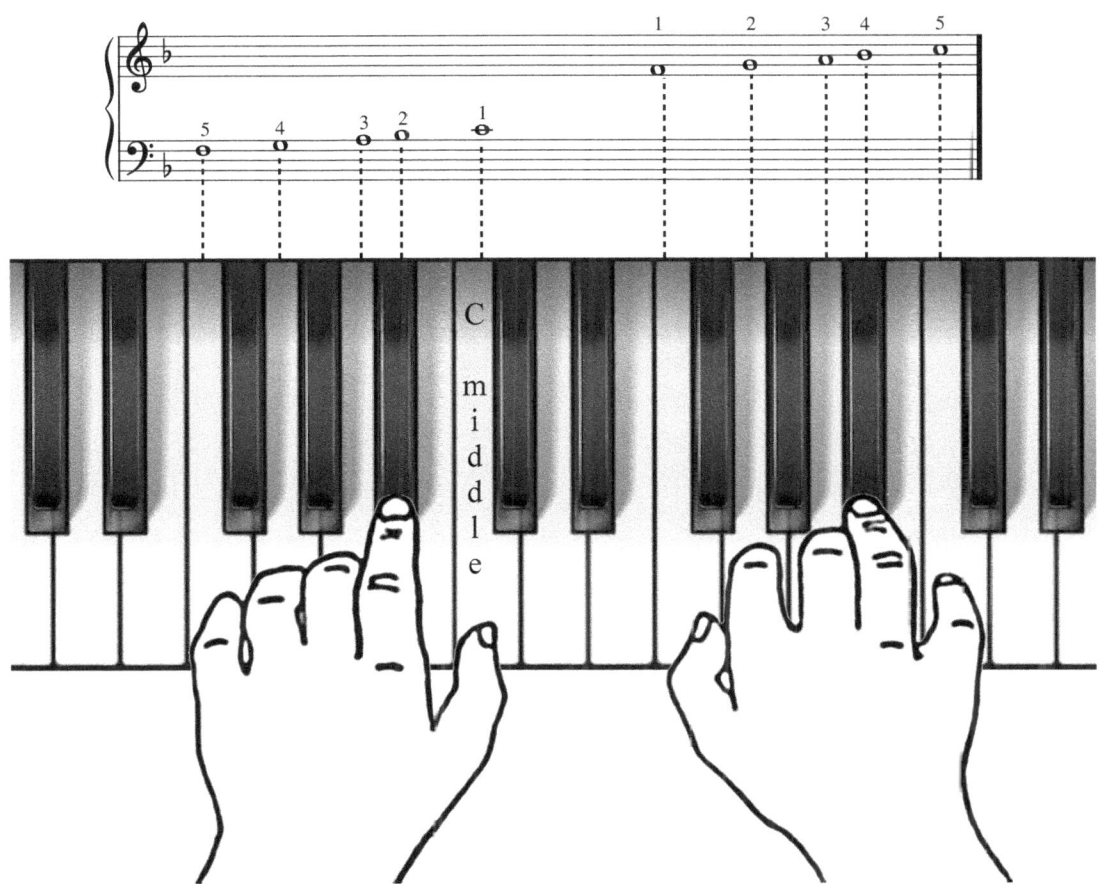

This arrangement of the fingers on the keys is called the "F major position". Why "major" is already known. It means "energetically, firmly'. And the note F is because the 1st finger of the right hand and the 5th finger of the left hand are ready to play the note F, which will now be found in the most important places of many pieces. On both staves, the same sign ♭ is displayed - "flat".

On the upper staff, it is on the 3rd line, which is occupied by the note B of the First octave. On the lower staff, it is on the 2nd line, which is also occupied by the note B (the note B of the Great Octave is written on the 2nd line of the lower staff. Since the "flat" signs are next to the keys of G and F, this means that they are valid throughout the entire piece. Therefore, from the 1st to the last measure, you need to play the note B-flat instead of the note B. In any measure, in any place in the piece and in any octave, you need to press the black key lying to the left instead of the white B key and lower the note B by half a tone. To make it easier to press the black keys, move the fingers of both hands a little closer to the black keys. But not too far forward, just enough to make it more comfortable for you.

When the "flat" sign is next to the key, it is not repeated in the notes anymore. You need to know and remember it from the very beginning of the piece. But sometimes the notes remind you of the sign when clef.

**Remember!** *If the "flat" or "sharp" signs are placed on the staff next to the "G" and "F" clefs, then they are called key signs and are valid throughout the entire piece.*

## 92. FOREST FLOWERS
### French song

**Calmly**

Arranged by J. Mercer

In the 1st, 3rd, 5th and 7th measures you see quarter notes with dots next to them on the right. These are "dotted quarter notes". The dot on the right affects the quarter note exactly the same as it does the half note - it lengthens the duration of the quarter note exactly by half. Everything works as in this picture. The duration of the dotted quarter note becomes equal to three eighth notes. Therefore, dotted quarter notes are counted exactly the same as eighth notes - an additional word "and" is added to each count: "One-and, two-and…".

Count the dotted quarter notes and press the keys as shown in these two pictures.

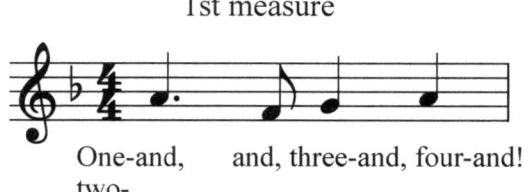

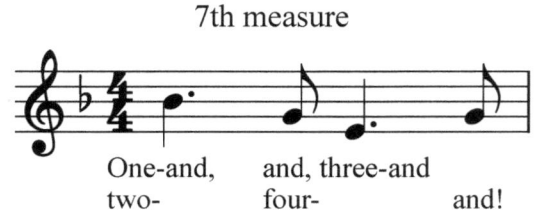

Hold the A key down for the count of "One-and, two." At the end of the count of "two," release the A key and press the F key for the count of "and".

Note: the eighth note that follows the dotted quarter note is pressed for the additional word "and".

Play B Flat with your right hand in the 2nd, 3rd, 5th, and 7th measures, and with your left hand in the 1st, 2nd, 3rd, 5th, 6th, and 7th measures.

## 93. ILLUSIONIST IN THE CIRCUS

**Moderately**

Arranged by J. Mercer

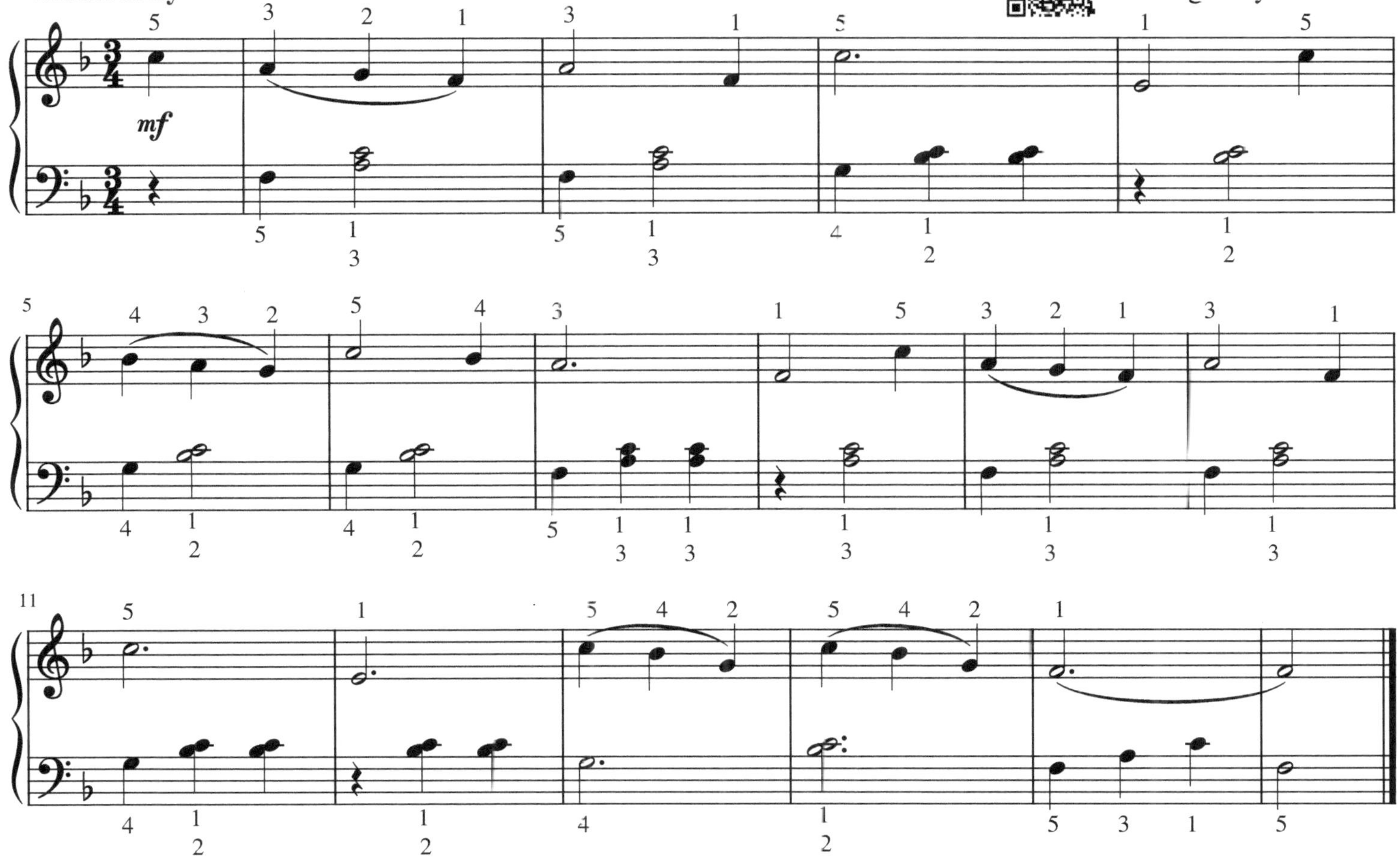

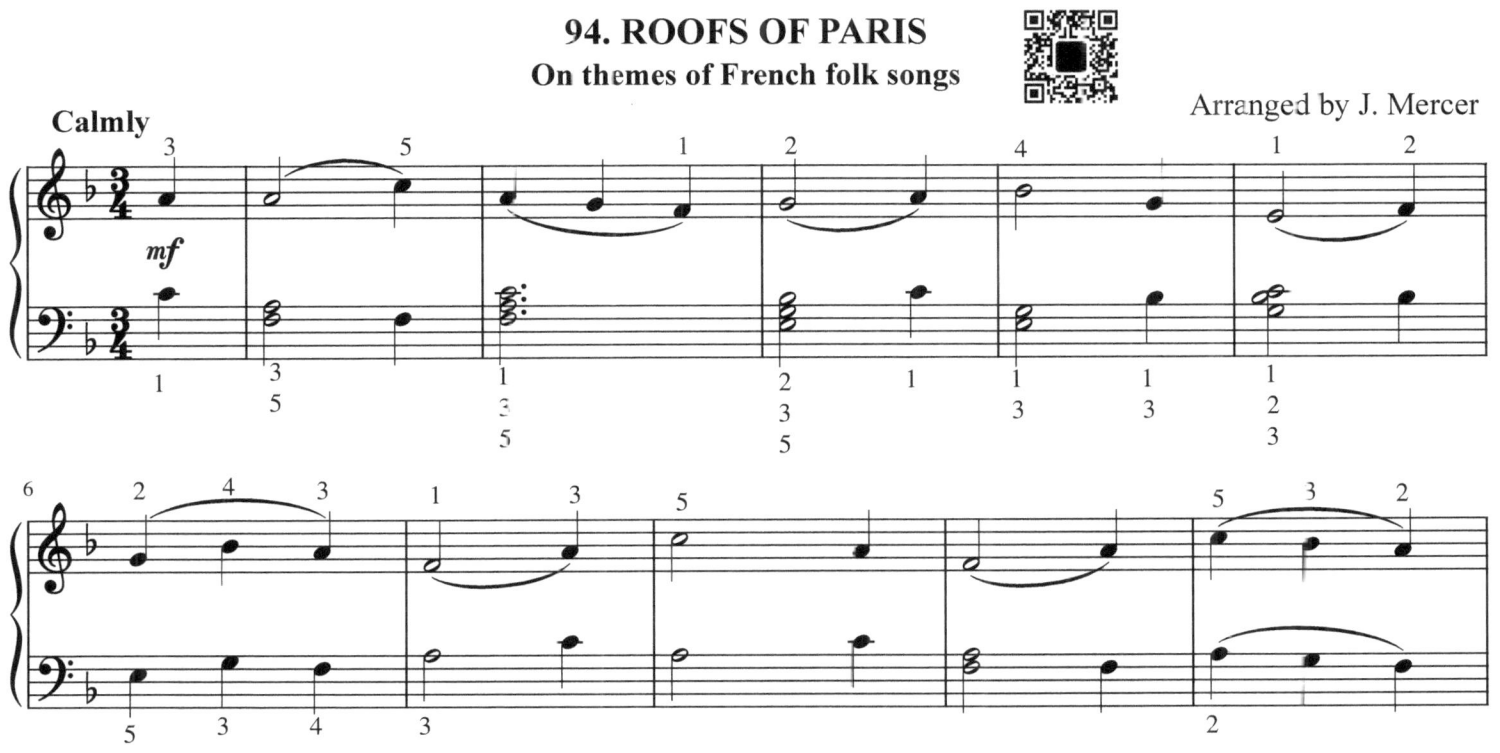

The melody of the piece begins with the pickup. Pay special attention to the even playing of both hands. B-flat for the right hand in the 6th, 7th, 14th and 15th measures, and for the left - in double notes in the 4th, 5th, 6th, 7th, 12th, 13th and 15th measures.

## 94. ROOFS OF PARIS

**On themes of French folk songs**

Arranged by J. Mercer

**Calmly**

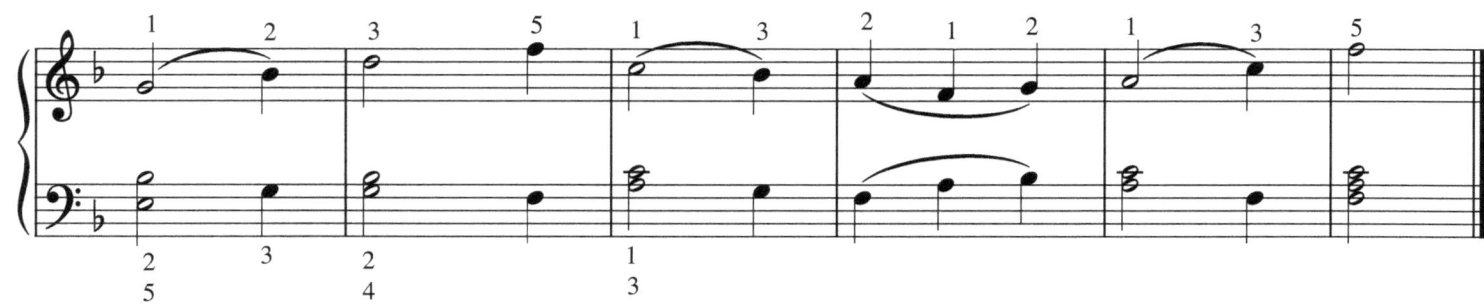

Play B-flat with your right hand in the 5th, 7th, 11th, 12th and 14th measures. Determine for yourself in which double notes, triads and chords you need to play B-flat with your left hand. In the 14th measure, move the 3rd finger of your right hand over the 1st.

## 95. BELLS ARE RINGING
### American New Year's Song

Arranged by J. Mercer

**Joyfully**

Learn a piece you already know with the F major hand position.

On the staves next to the notes there are flat signs, so throughout the piece you need to play the note B-flat instead of the note B. But in the 7th measure on the lower staff right before the note B of the minor octave there is a new sign ♮ . This sign is called NATURAL. It is placed in order to cancel the effect of the signs "flat" or "sharp". Therefore, in the 7th measure you must play not the note C-flat, but the note B, and press not the black, but the white key. The effect of the natural sign begins with the note before which it stands, and continues only until the end of the measure - until the new measure line. Consider that the natural sign, if it appears in any measure, has enough "power" only for this one measure. Therefore, in the 8th measure you should again play the note B-flat instead of the note B. The "flat" sign, which stands in the 8th measure before the note B, was not necessary to put. But it was put to remind about the "flat" sign, which is already next to the "F" clef.

In order to play the new piece correctly and smoothly, you need to learn to move the fourth finger over the first one right during the game, as if "crossing" these two fingers. Look how the pianist moves the fourth fingers in these two pictures.

Here the 4th finger of the right hand is transferred over the 1st finger

Here the 4th finger of the left hand is carried over the 1st finger

## 96. TWO SMALL EXERCISES

Hold the fingers of your right hand as shown in the picture. Play these exercises as many times as you can until you learn to smoothly move the 4th finger over the 1st, and smoothly - without tension and jerks - press the desired key with the 4th finger. At first, play the exercises slowly, and then increase the speed of the count and tempo as soon as you can. But only gradually. Do not forget the main thing: all the "work" is done by the fingers themselves. And the hand makes only a smooth and very light lateral movement towards the finger that is being moved.

Hold the fingers of your left hand as shown in the picture. Play these exercises exactly as you would the exercises for the fingers of your right hand.

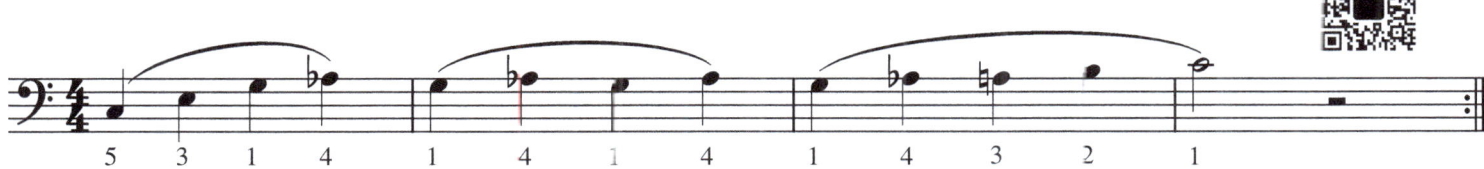

## 97. PILOT

Arranged by J. Mercer

In the 5th, 7th and 8th measures you see new signs under the upper staff. They look like a bell, a horn or a fork with two prongs: ———————— or ————————. These signs indicate how to change the volume of the sound while playing the piece. ———————— — this sign says that starting from the place where it stands, you need to gradually increase the volume of the play.

———————— — this sign says that starting from the place where it stands, you need to gradually decrease the volume.

Start playing the piece with medium volume — *mp*. But in the 5th, 6th and 7th measures, gradually increase the volume, and in the 8th measure, gradually decrease it, in order to finish the piece with the same volume — *mp*, with which it began. In the 5th and 7th measures on the lower staff before the note B of the small octave there is a natural sign. Therefore, instead of the note B-flat, play the note B in these measures. In the 1st, 3rd, 5th, 7th and 9th measures, move the 4th finger through the 1st.

## 98. CABARET
### Based on the dances in the Parisian cabaret "Moulin Rouge"

Arranged by J. Mercer

In the 2nd and 6th measures, place the 1st finger of your right hand under the 3rd finger, and in the 8th last measure, move the 4th finger of the same hand over the 1st finger.

## LEARN TO PLAY IN THE "G MAJOR" POSITION

Now you will become familiar with a new hand position. Distribute your fingers on the keys of the First and Small octaves as shown in the picture. Touch the keys with your fingertips.

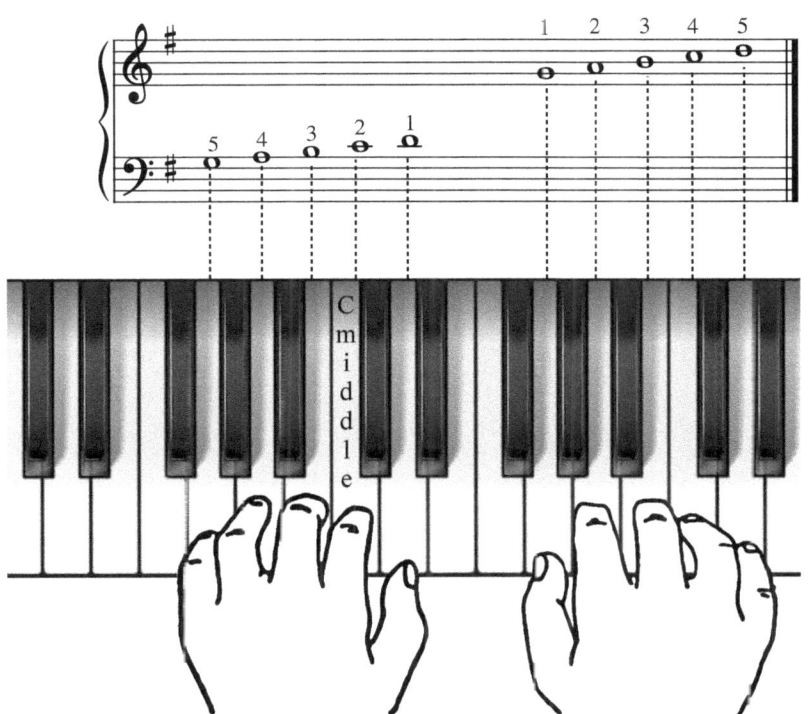

This arrangement of the fingers over the keys is called the G major position. The 1st finger of your right hand and the 5th finger of your left hand are ready to play the note G. Both staves have the same key sign ♯ — "sharp".

On the upper staff, it is on the 5th line, which is occupied by the note F of the Second Octave. On the lower staff, it is on the 4th line, which is also occupied by the note F of the Minor Octave. Since the "sharp" signs are next to the "G" and "F" notes, this means that they are valid throughout the entire piece - from the 1st to the last measure. Therefore, throughout the entire piece, you need to play the note F-sharp instead of the note F. In any measure, in any place in the piece and in any octave, you need to press the black key to the right instead of the white F key and play the note F-sharp.

To make it easier to press the black keys, move the fingers of both hands a little closer to the black keys, but not too far forward.

When the sharp sign is next to the clef, it is not repeated next to each F note. You need to know and remember it from the very beginning of the piece.

## 99. ROAD IN THE MOUNTAINS

Arranged by J. Mercer

**In the 3rd measure, play the note F-sharp with the 5th finger of your left hand.**

## 100. PONY

Arranged by J. Mercer

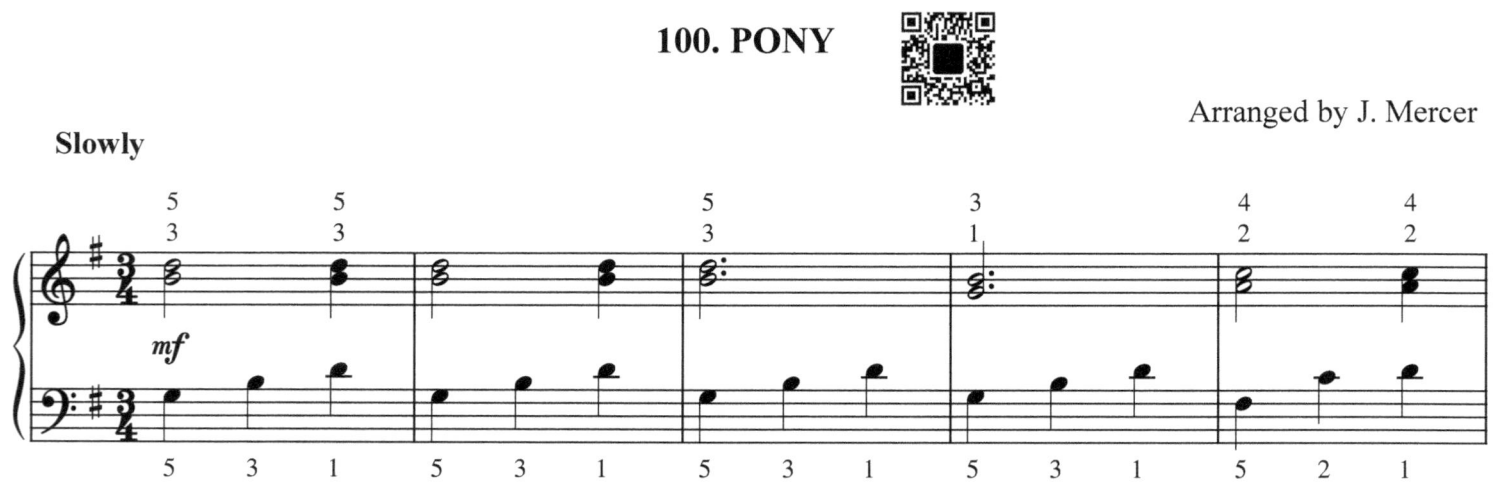

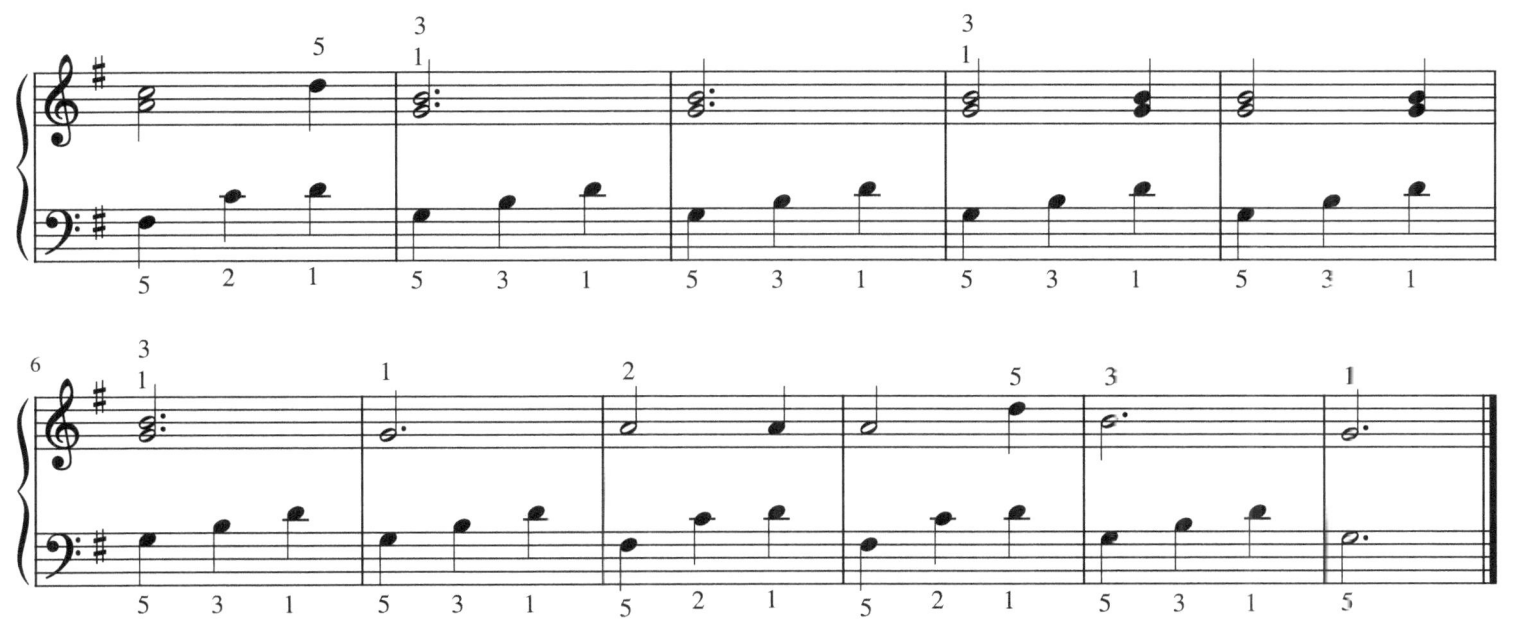

**Play with the hand position "G major" a piece you already know.**

## 101. BELLS ARE RINGING
### American New Year's song

Arranged by J. Mercer

**Joyfully**

*mf*

*f*

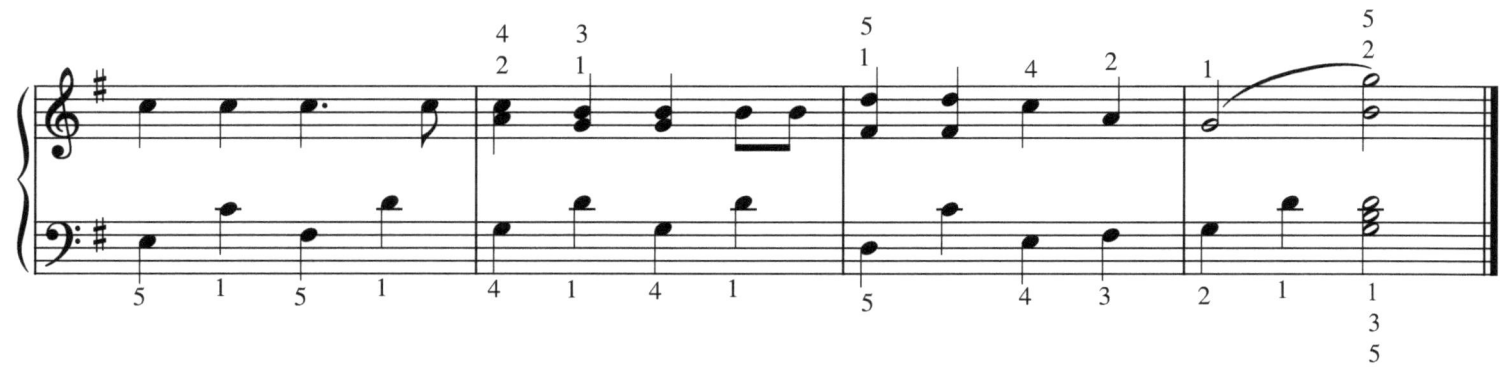

In the 4th and 12th measures, the natural signs before the F note cancel the effect of the key sharp sign. In the 7th measure, in the double notes on the lower staff, you need to play the C-sharp note twice in a row. In the 8th measure, the sharp sign no longer works, and you need to play the C note. But so that you don't mistakenly start playing the C-sharp note again, the natural sign is specially placed before the C note, although it is no longer needed there.

## 102. ON A MOTORCYCLE

Arranged by J. Mercer

**Moderately**

**At the end of the piece, in the 15th measure, play the note F-sharp with the 4th finger of the left hand.**

## 103. IN THE CLEAR MOON
**French folk song**

Arranged by J. Mercer

**Calmly**

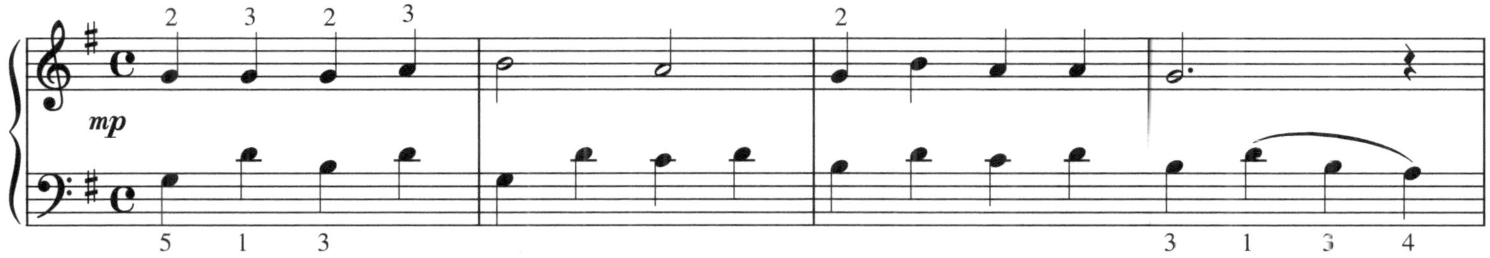

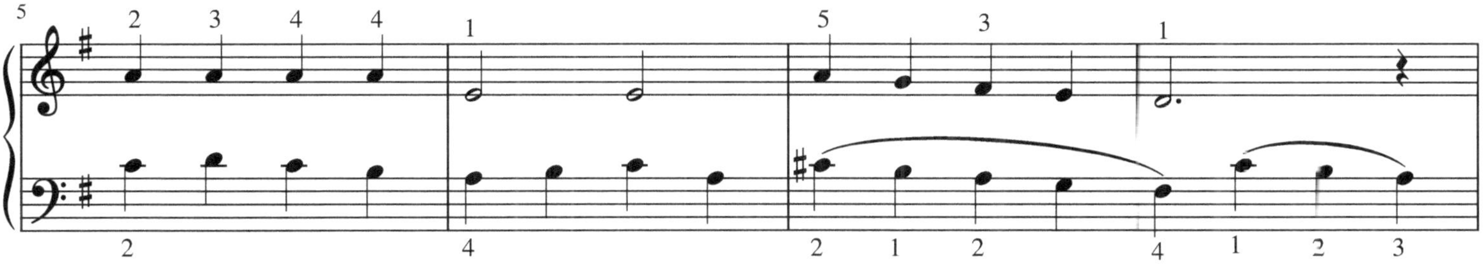

In the 1st, 5th and 9th measures, the adjacent identical notes - G and A - are best played with different fingers. In the 7th measure, play the note F-sharp with the 3rd finger of the right hand, and in the 8th measure, play the note F-sharp of the minor octave with the 4th finger of the left hand. In the 7th measure, press the black key with the 2nd finger of the left hand and play the note C-sharp, and at the same time, place the 1st finger under the 2nd in advance, so that you have time to press the next key smoothly and play B.

# 104. HORSE RIDE

Arranged by J. Mercer

**Moderately**

With your left hand, play the note F-sharp in the 3rd, 4th, 5th, 9th, 15th and 16th measures. With the 2nd finger of your right hand, play F-sharp in the 16th measure. In the 10th measure, play the note C-sharp, and in the 11th measure, play this note on both staves at once. In the 12th and 13th measures, the tie connects two identical D notes. Therefore, you press the D key with the 5th finger only once - in the 12th measure - and hold it down for two full measures - the 12th and 13th.

# 105. OLD CAR

**Moderately**

Arranged by J. Mercer

The note F sharp appears on the upper staff in measures 2, 6, and 14, and on the lower staff in measures 3, 4, 7, and 15. Count and play the dotted quarter notes carefully.

# LEARN TO PLAY AND HOLD YOUR FINGERS IN DIFFERENT POSITIONS

You have already understood that the placement of your fingers on the keys depends on the notes in which the piece is written. Therefore, a pianist must be able to quickly and smoothly change the position of his fingers on the keys.

But no matter what position the fingers are in, they should always be slightly ROUNDED, relaxed, and move easily and freely.

## 106. ON THE TOP OF THE MOUNTAIN
### American traditional song

Arranged by J. Mercer

First of all, correctly determine the durations of identical adjacent notes connected by a separate ligature. Remember: the first connected note "takes" the durations of the others and sounds "one for all". For example, in the 4th and 5th measures, the note A will sound for only 5 beats, in the 7th, 8th and 9th measures, the note G will sound for only 8 beats. Calculate in advance how long the remaining identical notes connected by a separate ligature will sound.

## 107. TYROLIAN WALTZ
### On themes of Tyrolean melodies

Arranged by J. Mercer

**Slowly**

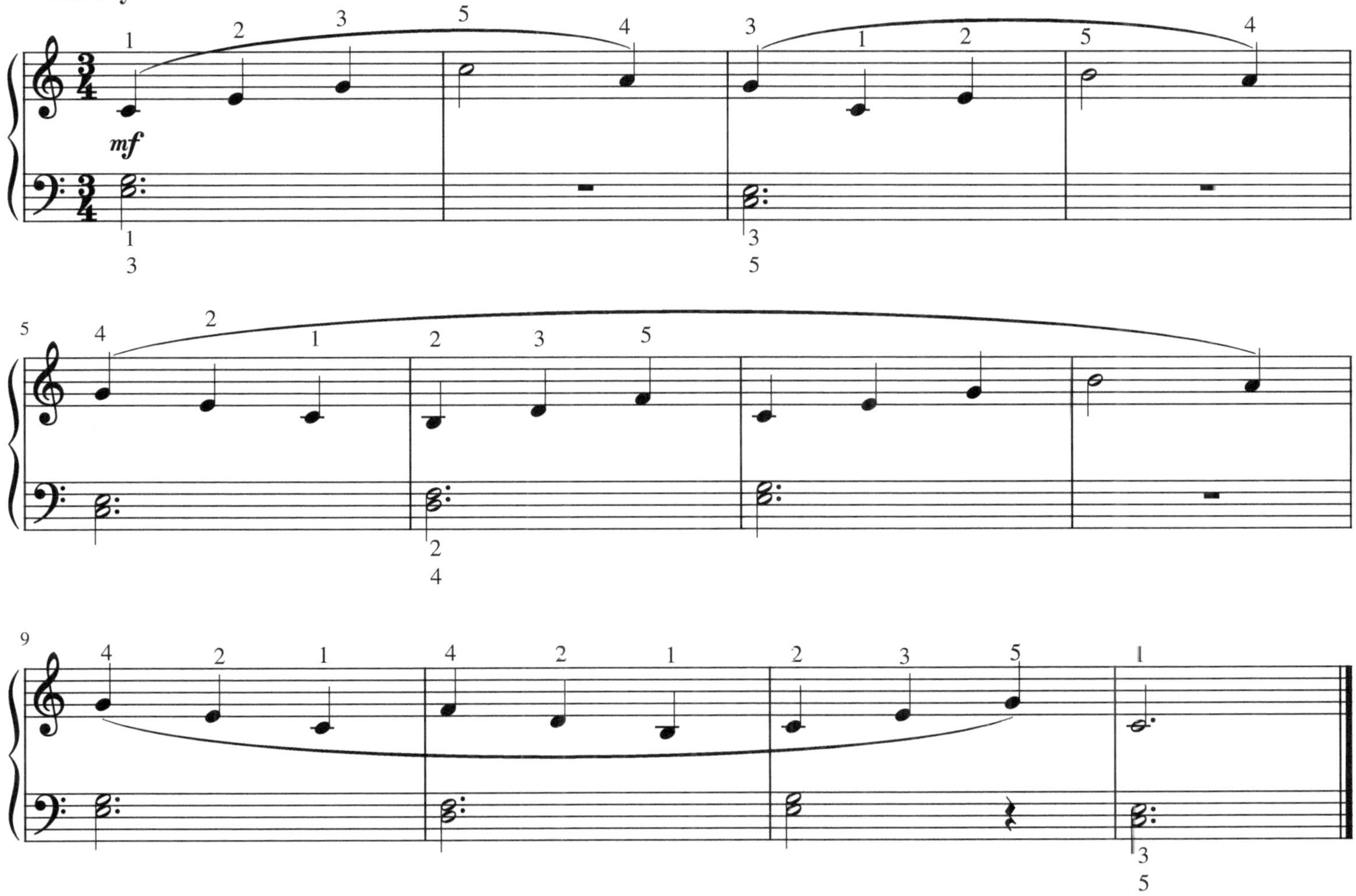

Play this waltz more often, and your fingers will gradually stretch and cover more keys on the keyboard. In the 6th measure, move the 2nd finger of the right hand over the 1st finger.

# 108. THE ORGAN PLAYS

**Moderately slow**

Arranged by J. Mercer

Play this piece slowly and solemnly, because this is how a real organ sounds in a large hall. Increase and decrease the volume where it is indicated in the notes. In the 12th measure on the lower staff between the 1st and 2nd lines you see a note that you have not played before. This is the note A of the Great Octave. Press the 2nd key to the left of the C of the Small Octave.

# 109. ROBOTS ON A WALK

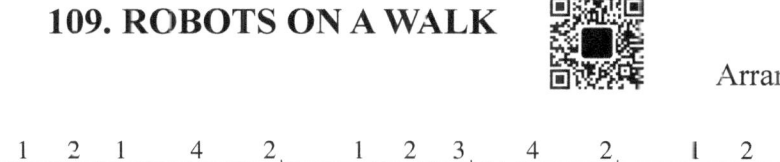

Arranged by J. Mercer

In the 13th and 14th measures there are two small crossed out notes: B-flat and G. These notes are called "Grace Note", which means "pre-accent". They are called so because individual durations are not counted for them, they are not stressed, and they are played at the expense of the duration of the note before which they stand. The grace note simply "steals" a little duration from the note before which it stands, but in return it decorates this note. It turns out that instead of one note, two sound: first, the grace note sounds very briefly, and immediately after it, the main note sounds. The grace note must be played very quickly and easily. Therefore, practice at first: lightly strike the G key with the 4th finger, as if you were striking a match, and immediately "step over" to the A key with the 5th finger. Play the grace note in B-flat exactly like this. "Strike" the black key with the 3rd finger and immediately move the 2nd finger to the A key.

Before playing the piece, remember how robots walk in movies. For example, how the 'robot policeman" walks. That's how you play it!

# 110. FOREST ELF

Arranged by J. Mercer

In all measures except the 4th, you must play alternately both staccato and legato. In the 2nd, 3rd and 4th measures, on the lower staff there are notes that you seem to have never encountered before. But in fact, these notes are very familiar to you. These are the notes D, E and F of the First Octave, which have moved from the upper staff to the lower one so that you can play them with your left hand.

See how in this picture the notes move from the upper staff to the lower one, and how they are written in a new way on the lower staff.

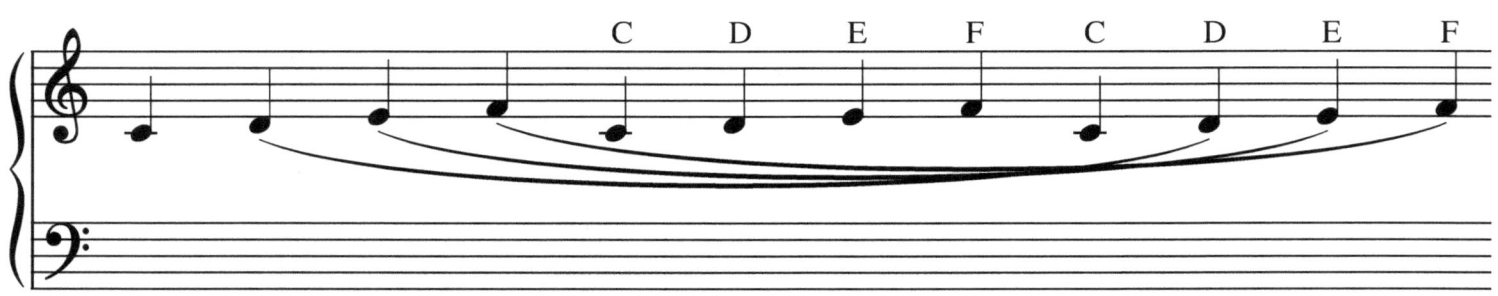

In the 4th measure, play D-sharp with the 2nd finger of your left hand. Play the piece with medium volume — *mf* , and in the 2nd and 6th measures, stress the note E, because there are accent marks above these notes. In the 4th measure, on the lower staff, there is a note D-sharp of the first octave. Press the black key with the 2nd finger of your left hand.

# 111. OLD FRIENDSHIP
## Scottish folk song

Arranged by J. Mercer

**Slowly**

*mp*

The melody of this song is built from long and smooth musical phrases. Therefore, you need to play the piece slowly - at a medium tempo and with a medium volume: at the beginning, a little quieter, in the middle, a little louder, and at the end, a little less. To make the legato playing smoother, try to change fingers for the same notes if they are next to each other. For example. in the 2nd measure, play the F note first with the 4th, then the 3rd and 2nd finger.

## 112. WALTZ OF THE FIGURE DANCERS

Arranged by J. Mercer

**Slowly**

On the upper staff in the 3rd and 4th measures, two A notes are connected by a common slur. This means that you only need to press the A key once, and the A note will sound for two full measures - all 6 quarter notes. In exactly the same way, two B notes are connected by a common slur in the 7th and 8th measures.

## 113. GYMNAST ON THE TRAPEZE
### Circus song

Arranged by J. Mercer

**Slowly, quietly**

In the 16th measure on the upper staff you see the designation "1-3" above the note G. It turns out that this note should be played with two fingers at once - the 1st and 3rd. In fact, you press the G key with only the 1st finger. And then, without releasing the G key, you change the 1st finger to the 3rd right on the key. While the note G sounds for 3 whole quarters, you will have enough time to do this. But now it will be convenient for you to play the double note "G-D" in the 17th last measure. Learn to smoothly and imperceptibly change fingers on the same key.

## 114. AROUND THE MOUNTAIN
### American traditional song

Arranged by J. Mercer

At the very beginning of the 2nd measure, under the quarter note G, you see a double whole note B-D. You have never seen such an arrangement of notes on one staff. This notation of notes is used to indicate a special, very important and interesting technique of playing the piano, which is called "playing with one hand in the first and second voices." Learn to do this. On the count of "one," you press three keys at once with the 1st, 2nd and 4th fingers: B of the Small Octave, D and G. With the 1st and 2nd fingers, you hold down the double whole note B-D for all four counts. At the same time, without releasing these two keys B and D, you press the G key 3 more times with only the 4th finger on the count - "two, three, four!" It turns out that you play the melody with the 4th finger, and the 1st and 2nd fingers play the accompaniment with the second voice. Also hold down the B note in the 3rd measure and the double note D-G in the 6th measure. In the 11th measure, the held half note F will sound only for the first two quarter notes of the measure. On the count of "three" you should remove your first finger from this key and no longer hold the note F. *Pay attention and remember!* The notes that record the second voice and the notes that record the main melody have "sticks" pointing in opposite directions. This is done to distinguish one voice from the other. In the 4th, 5th, 16th, 17th and 18th measures, you will play the second voice only with individual quarter notes. Just like for the main melody, the second voice has its own rests in the notes. You can see these quarter rests in the 4th, 5th, 11th, 16th, 17th and 18th measures.

In the 17th and the last 19th measure, on the 1st line of the lower staff there is a note G of the Great Octave, which should be played with the 5th finger.

Pay attention to the sharp sign in the 7th measure before the note C. In the 8th measure there is a natural sign before this note, but this sign is just for reminder. But in the 15th measure, before the second note C, the natural sign is very necessary. It cancels the effect of the sharp standing before the first note C. In the 11th measure, the natural sign before the note of the upper voice F cancels the effect of the sharp sign. In the 13th measure, playing the double note B-flat - C-sharp, press two black keys at once with the 1st and 5th fingers of your left hand.

## 115. DOVE, COME FLY
### German folk song

Arranged by J. Mercer

The melody of the song consists of two phrases that need to be played "legato". The piece begins with an incomplete measure - the pickup. Therefore, in the 1st measure, you do not need to make an accent, but on the contrary - you need to play the first two eighth notes with light presses on the keys. Then the 1st measure will be light, like the flap of a dove's wing. In the 3rd and 7th measures, the same notes D are next to each other. It is better to play them with different fingers. Learn to smoothly step onto the same key with different fingers.

With your left hand, play one common "legato" for all measures.

## 116. THE FIRST CHRISTMAS
### American Traditional Song

Arranged by J. Mercer

125

The piece consists of long phrases that need to be played "legato". So smoothly "step-step" from finger to finger. In the last measure, above the last two notes there is a new sign for you — 𝄐. This sign is called FERMATA, which in Italian means "stop" or "pause". So you need to hold the keys down until the sound gradually stops on its own. The duration of the notes themselves, above which there is a "fermata" sign, is not particularly important.

## 117. CAT ON A HOT ROOF

Arranged by J. Mercer

**Lively, movably**

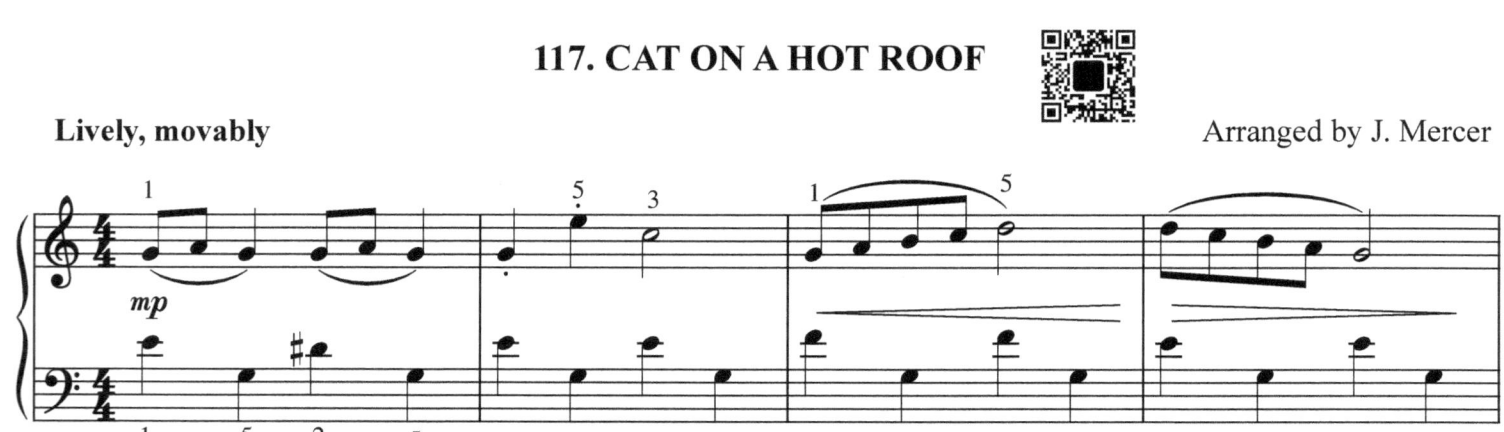

This piece uses all three playing styles: legato, non-legato and staccato. In the first eight measures, the left hand plays both the Minor and the First Octave. In the Minor Octave, you press only the G key with your 5th finger. And in the First Octave, you press the notes E, D-sharp, F with your 1st and 2nd fingers, and in the 8th measure, you play the double note C-E with two fingers at once - the 1st and 3rd. In the 9th and 10th measures, the ligature unites the notes of the lower and upper staff. This means that when playing legato, you must "pass" it from your left hand to your right. In the 10th measure, the Treble clef appears on the lower staff. This is done to make it easier to find and play the notes of the First Octave with your left hand. In the 11th measure, the Bass clef returns to its place. In the 7th measure, playing the note C, place the 1st finger of your right hand under the 3rd.

## 118. DANCE OF THE INDIAN CHIEFS

### Part I

Arranged by J. Mercer

## Part II

The dance should be played very evenly and at a fast tempo. The accompaniment of double quarter notes will help you play evenly: A (Big Octave) - E (Small Octave).

This accompaniment does not change from the beginning to the end of the piece and resembles the dull, even beats of Indian war drums. In addition, in almost every measure, you need to emphasise the first quarter - the strong beat of the measure. Starting from the 3rd measure, the note sign — appears in the notes. These notes must be played especially clearly. The key must be pressed vigorously and the full duration of the note must be maintained.

The piece is played loudly, and only from the 9th measure the volume of the sound decreases to average. But then from the 16th measure the volume gradually increases, and from the 19th measure it increases even more. and at the end the dance sounds very loud.

In the first two measures of the second part of the piece, pay attention to the staccato playing.

You have to learn this dance so well that you can then play it all evenly in 40 seconds.

# 119. CHANCE ENCOUNTER

**Moderately**

Arranged by J. Mercer

In the 1st, 3rd, 5th, 7th, 9th, 11th and 13th measures, the 1st finger of the right hand is placed under the 2nd finger. Before learning and playing the piece, play each of these measures separately and practice until you begin to place the 1st finger easily, freely and without straining your fingers and hand. From the 9th to the 12th measure, the Bass clef gives way to the Treble clef on the lower staff. You will play these measures with both your right and left hands in the same Treble clef. This is done to make it easier to find and play the notes of the First Octave with your left hand. From the 13th measure, the Bass clef returns to the lower staff. Pay special attention: in the piece, the volume of the sound constantly changes - from *mf* to *p*, then to *f*, and then again to *mf*.

# 120. HAPPY NEW YEAR
## American Traditional Song

Arranged by J. Mercer

The entire piece, except for the 4th, 8th and 12th measures, is played non legato. In the 1st, 5th, 9th, 10th and 13th measures, try to play the same notes next to each other with different fingers. In the 3rd and 11th measures, press the D key with the 1st finger of your right hand and hold it down for a whole measure - all four counts. At the same time, play quarter notes of F with the 3rd finger. In the 12th and 15th measures, play two half notes with the second voice. Don't forget: the "sticks" of the notes of the second voice are directed in the opposite direction. Pay attention to the 7th measure: there are two "natural" signs on the lower staff. The first natural sign before the B note cancels the effect of the flat sign, which is next to the clef. But the natural sign before the F note cancels the effect of the sharp sign, which also appeared before the F note, but only on the upper staff. Therefore, in this measure, you play the black F-sharp key with your right hand, and play the white F key with your left hand. In the 10th measure, with the 3rd and 1st fingers of your left hand, you first simultaneously press the black and white keys C-sharp and E, and then, in exactly the same way, with the 3rd and 2nd fingers, you press two black keys C-sharp and E-flat, since the sharp sign is valid throughout the entire measure.

# 121. HOME TO FLORIDA

Arranged by J. Mercer

**Moderately**

In many measures - in the 1st, 3rd, 5th, 6th and others - you need to smoothly place the 1st finger under the 3rd and transfer the 3rd finger over the 1st. Always remember: the main beauty and charm of playing the piano is the smooth and easy "legato" play of long and beautiful musical phrases.

In the 11th and 12th measures, two ligatures connect two identical double notes standing next to each other. I remind you: you do not play the second double note, but count its sound.

## 122. GOAT ON THE RAILS
### Student song

Arranged by J. Mercer

This is a special piece. It will teach you to play both the melody and the accompaniment with your left hand at the same time. So forget about your right hand for a while, and play the whole piece only with your left hand.

You play with your left hand on two staves at once - in the key of "G" and in the key of "F". The finger numbers on both staves are indicated only for the left hand.

The piece has many chords that will help you "stretch" the fingers of your left hand a little. But you should not strain your fingers and hand too much when playing the chords. Try especially not to strain the 1st and 5th fingers. Keep your hand and hand as free and relaxed as possible.

When playing the chords, try to prepare your fingers in advance - while still in the air, so that it is easier to hit the right keys. Be sure to make sure that the 5th finger presses the key with its tip, and not with its side.

It is better to learn the piece slowly and in parts - two or three measures.

At the end of the piece there is a reprise - a sign of repetition. Keep in mind: It is always useful to repeat this piece.

## 123. TRAIN TO THE RIVIERA

Arranged by J. Mercer

**Calmly**

The right hand plays short phrases written in eighth notes "legato". These phrases depict the movement of a train that is slowly approaching a famous seaside resort. The left hand plays quarter and half notes, which depict the whistles given by the locomotive engineer. On the lower staff in each measure there are two notes. The first note is a quarter note, written in the clef of F. The second note is a half note, written in the Treble clef. Both notes are to be played with the left hand. The Treble clef on the lower staff is needed to make it easier to find and play the notes of the First and Second Octaves with the left hand. All notes on the lower staff, preceded by the Treble clef, should be played by moving the left hand over the right. And all these notes should be played with an increased accent. For example, in the 1st measure you play C of the Small Octave with your left hand, and then you move your left hand over your right hand and play the C of the Second Octave with an accent.

The ∧ (or ∨) sign in the notes indicates an increased accent.

## 124. SILENT NIGHT

Arranged by J. Mercer

In the 1st, 3rd, 5th, 7th, 11th, 13th and 14th measures, there are dotted half notes with the "sticks" pointing downwards on the upper staff. These are "delayed" notes that should sound in the second voice. The duration of a dotted half note is equal to three quarter notes, so the "delayed" notes should sound throughout the entire measure. On the count of "one", you press the "delayed" note and hold it down for two more counts - "two, three". And then this note sounds in the second voice for the entire measure - all three counts. And while the "delayed" note sounds, you press the notes of the first voice with the free fingers of your right hand and play the main melody. Watch the changes in volume indicated in the notes.

# 125. THE SPARROW

Arranged by J. Mercer

**Lively**

With the right and left hand, all quarter notes should be played "staccato" - exactly like a 10-gram jump on the asphalt by sparrows. In the 3rd and 7th measures, play the F-sharp note with the 2nd finger of the right hand, In the 2nd, 4th, 6th, 8th, 11th and 15th measures, play the F-sharp foot of the Small Octave with the 5th finger of the left hand, and in the last - 16th measure - play this note with the 4th finger.

# 126. CABARET
## Based on the dances in the Parisian cabaret "Moulin Rouge"

Arranged by J. Mercer

**Joyfully**

This piece is familiar to you, but now you will play it with a different accompaniment.

Note what groups of notes are written: for every quarter note in the right hand there are two eighth notes in the left, and for every half note there are four eighth notes, connected by one common LINING ("crossbar").

# 127. RAILROAD
## American Traditional Song

Arranged by J. Mercer

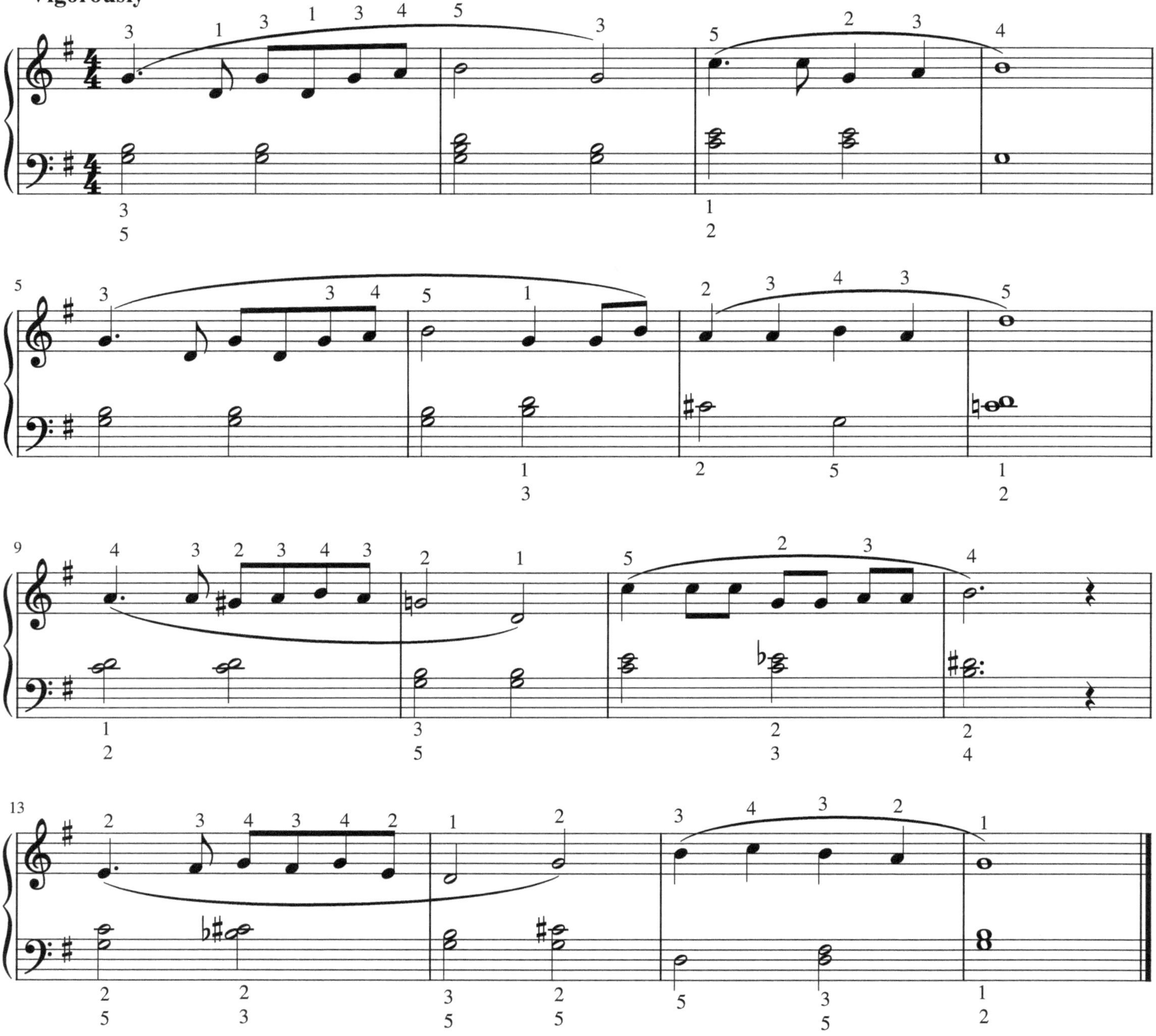

The natural signs in measures 8 and 10 are there only to remind you that the sharp signs that appeared in measures 7 and 9 are no longer effective in the next measure. Note the double notes in measures 11 and 12. The E-flat note in measure 11 and the D-sharp note in measure 12 are played on the same black key. Therefore, you play both of these notes with the 2nd finger of your left hand and press the same black key.

# 128. AUTUMN MELODY

Arranged by J. Mercer

In the 13th measure, play the note F-sharp with the 2nd finger of the right hand and at the same time put the 1st finger under the 2nd in advance, so that you can play the note G in time and smoothly. The main difficulty for you in this piece is to change the fingers of the left hand in time and correctly, so that you can play the double notes of the accompaniment evenly. The melody is very beautiful - so practice!

## 129. HUMPTY DUMPTY
### English song

Arranged by J. Mercer

**Joyfully**

In this piece the size of the measures is indicated by numbers: $\frac{3}{8}$, read and pronounced - "three eighths". Measures with the size of " $\frac{3}{8}$ " are very similar to measures with the size of " $\frac{3}{4}$ ". These are also triple measures and therefore are also counted in three counts: "one, two, three". But the number "8" says that in measures with the size of " $\frac{3}{8}$ " one beat is taken not one quarter note, but one eighth note. Therefore, in these measures, each eighth note is counted in one count - "one", and each quarter note is counted in two counts - "one, two". The dotted quarter note is counted in three counts and sounds one full measure.

Starting from the 17th measure, a dotted quarter note G appears, and then - F, which should be played by the second voice.

## 130. TRADITIONAL CANADIAN WALTZ

Arranged by J. Mercer

**In waltz tempo, with feeling**

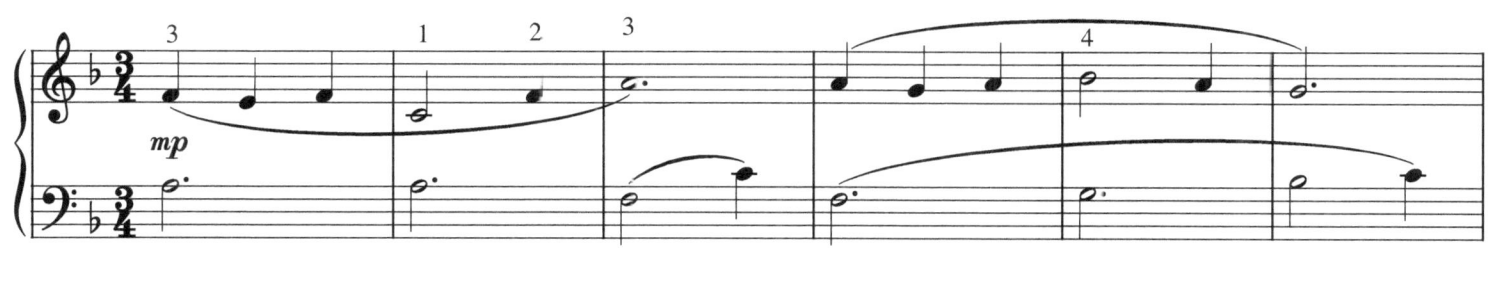

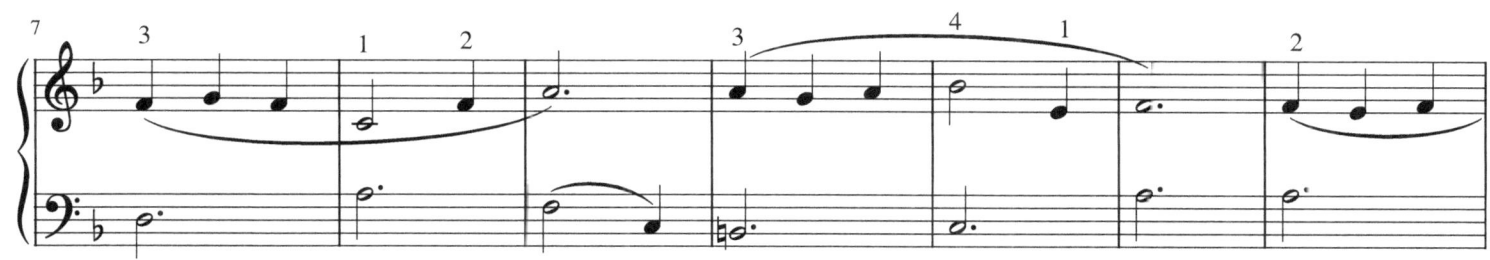

## 131. ON ONE FINE DAY
### From the opera "Madame Butterfly"

Arranged by J. Mercer

**Slowly, with feeling**

# 132. GOLDFISHES
### English song

**Moderately and slowly**

Arranged by J. Mercer

In this piece the size of the measures is indicated by numbers: $\frac{6}{8}$, read and pronounced - "six eighths"
This is a complex measure, which was obtained by combining two simple triple measures of $\frac{3}{8}$ each:

**Simple triple** + **Simple triple** = **Complex six-beat measure**

A six-beat measure consists of six beats. Each beat is one eighth note, which is counted on one count: "One!" The entire measure is counted on the count: "One, two, three, four, five, six!"

The first and fourth beats in a six-beat measure are strong, but only the fourth beat is weaker than the first. But the second, third, fifth and sixth beats in this measure are weak, since they were weak in their three-beat measures.

142

# 133. CANCAN (GALLOP)
## From the operetta "Orpheus in the Underworld"

Arranged by J. Mercer

**Fast**

# 134. WALTZ OF THE LITTLE FAIRY

Arranged by J. Mercer

**In waltz tempo, with tenderness**

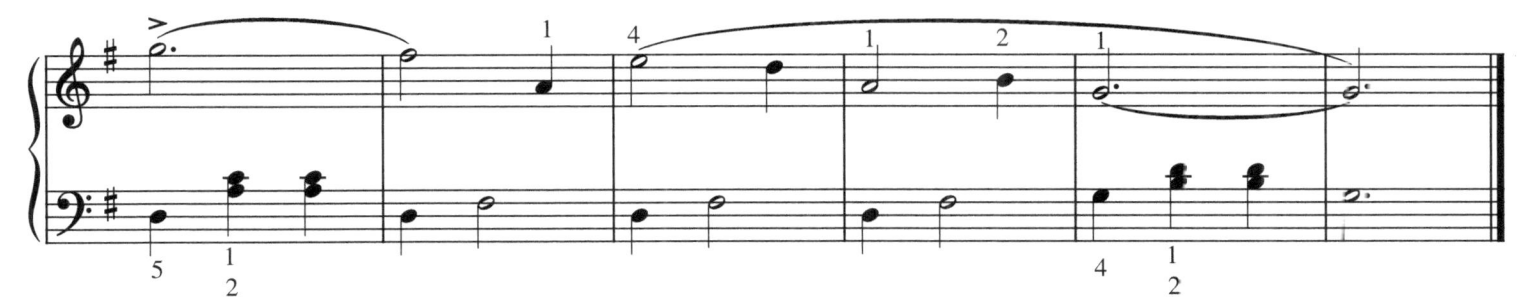

## 135. WALTZ DANCING BEARS
### German folk melody

In waltz tempo

Arranged by J. Mercer

# 136. POLKA

Arranged by J. Mercer

**Lively**

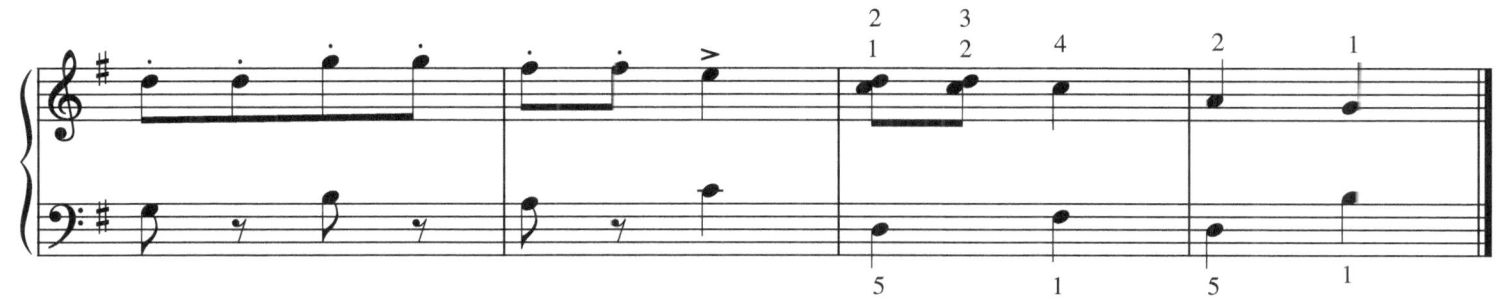

## 137. TA-RA-RA BOOM-DI-HEY!
### Pop song

Arranged by J. Mercer

**Joyfully**

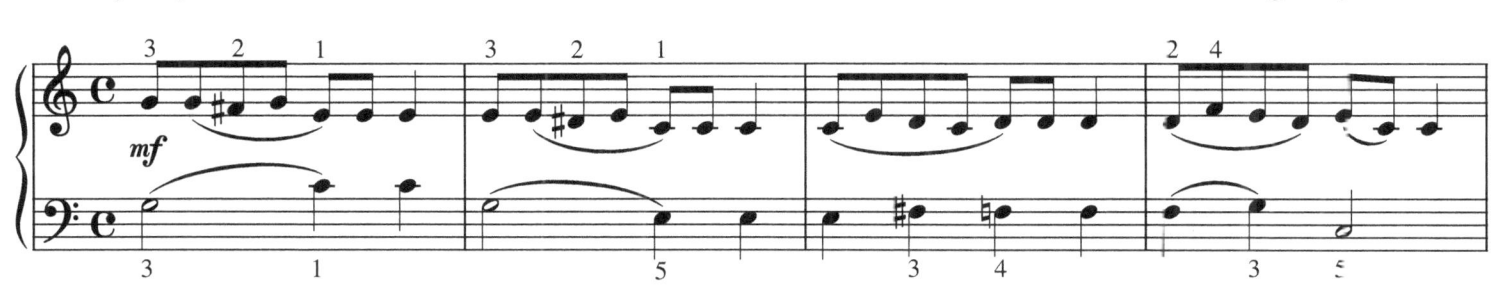

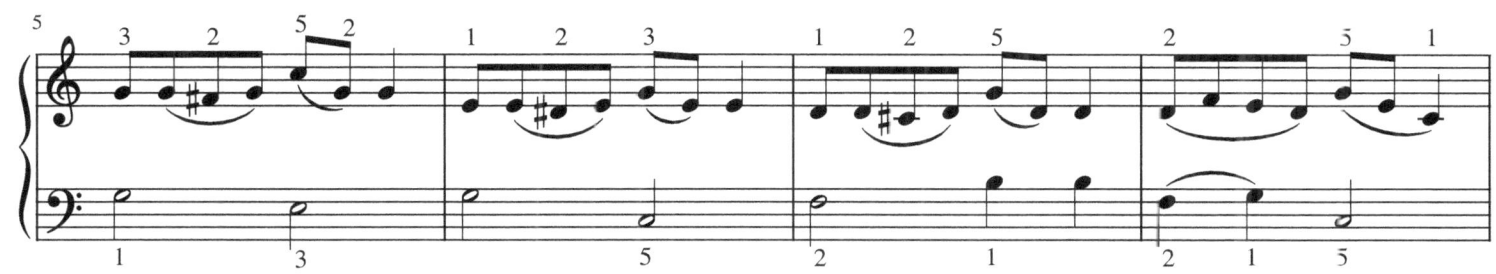

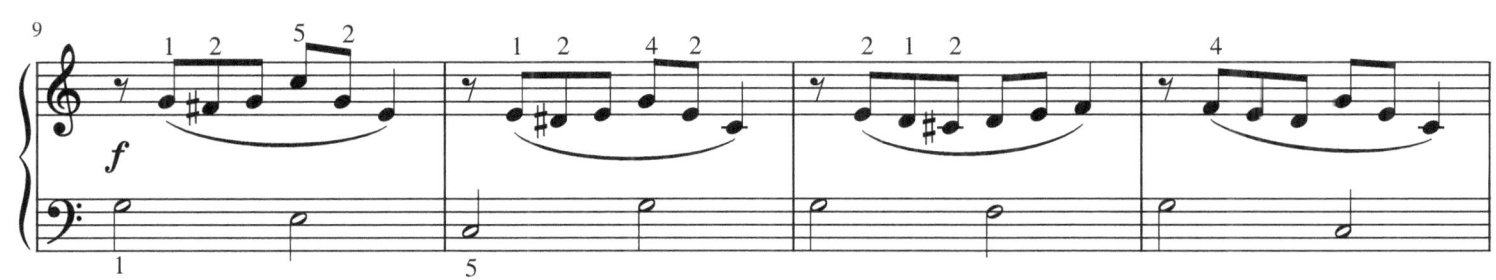

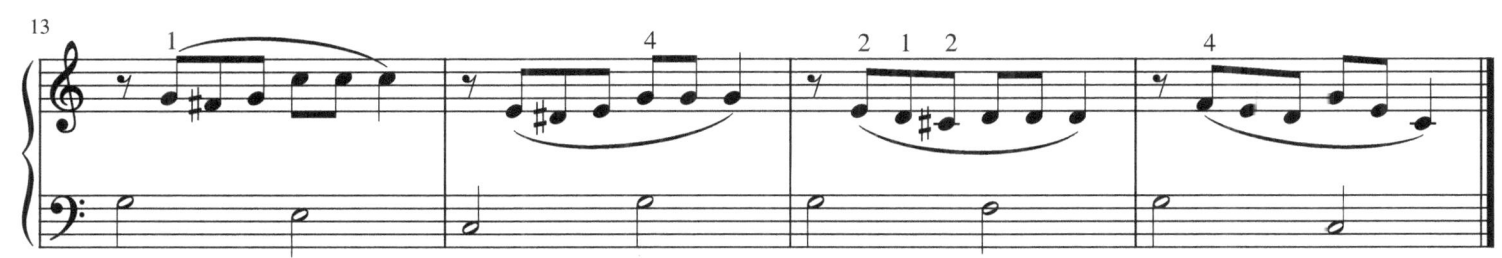

## 138. WALTZ-INTERMEZZO
### From the operetta "The Merry Widow"

Arranged by J. Mercer

**In waltz tempo**

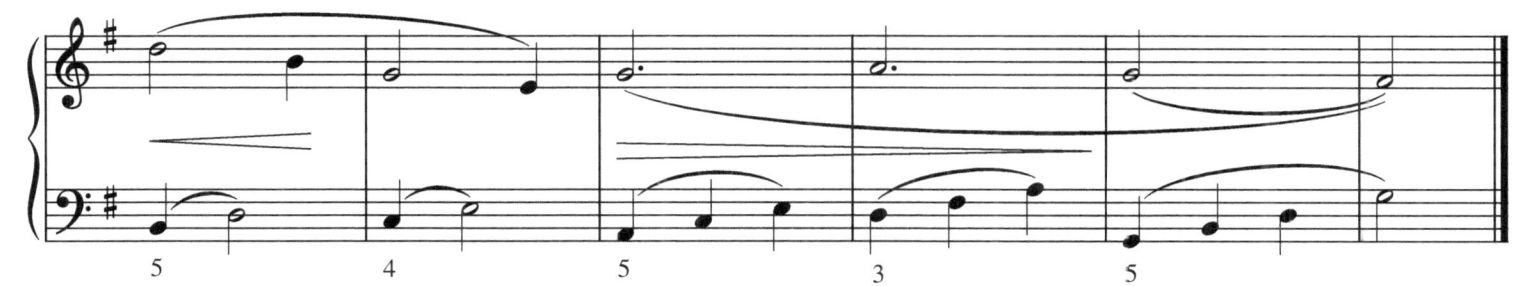

## 139. O SOLE MIO
### Italian (Neapolitan) song

Arranged by J. Mercer

**Chantly with great feeling**

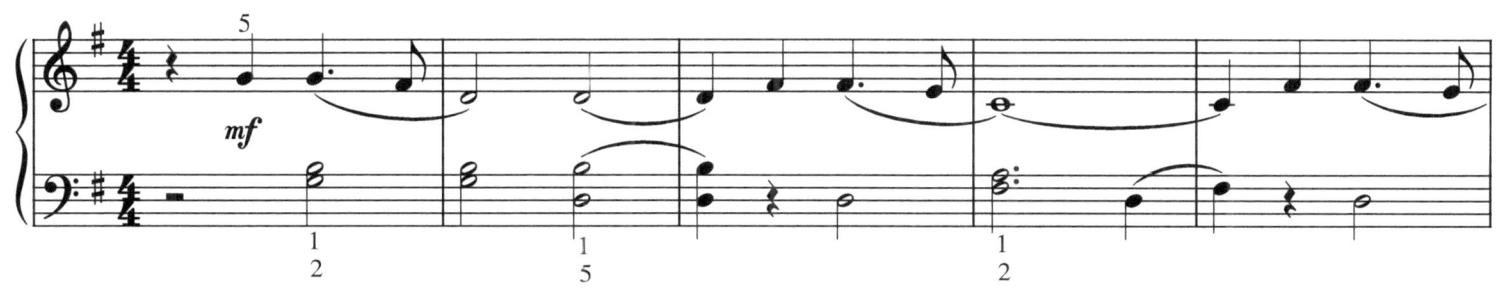

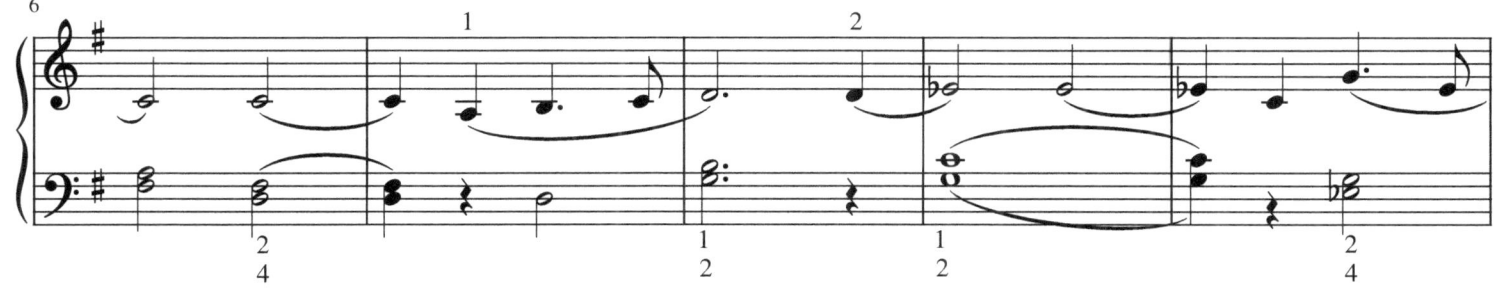

# 140. NEW YORK SIDEWALKS

**Easy and fun**

Arranged by J. Mercer

Piano Course Book For Beginners: Teach yourself how to read music, play famous piano songs, educational and methodological manual.

VIDEO LESSONS INCLUDED -- Watch the Notes Fall, Then Play
Every song comes with a companion falling notes video lesson (Synthesia-style) showing the notes dropping in real time.

Piano Course: 140 new pieces for students of preparatory, first and second grades of children's music schools: teaching aid / author-compiler Julian Mercer.

"Piano Course" meets all the requirements for publications for junior grades of children's music schools as a teaching aid.

"Piano Course" successfully combines an original method of explaining fundamental musical concepts with a modern method of practical teaching of piano playing.

A distinctive feature of "Piano Course" is its repertoire, composed of pieces and arrangements of folk and original music from Western European and North American countries.

ISBN 979-8-218-63461-2

# FREE BONUS BOOK!